FRANKIE

EDITED BY
BROUGH SCOTT
RACING POST

Half-title: flying dismount from Foundation after the Royal Lodge Stakes, 2015. Frontispiece: winning the 2007 Derby on Authorized.

First published in Great Britain in 2015 by
Racing Post Books
27 Kingfisher Court, Hambridge Road, Newbury, Berkshire, RG14 5SJ

10 9 8 7 6 5 4 3 2 1

ISBN 978-1-910498-30-9

Cover designed by Jay Vincent
Text designed by J Schwartz & Co.

Printed and bound in Italy by L.E.G.O. S.p.A

www.racingpost.com/shop

Photographic Acknowledgements
All the photos are copyright © Racing Post except the following:
Colin Russell: page 136
Cranhamphotos: pages 35, 56-7, 60, 72, 181, 197 top, 263
Daily Telegraph/Paul Grover: page 51
Dan Abraham: page 140
Getty Images: pages 123, 151, 163, 223, 228, 233, 235, 254 top, 265, 268
Martin Lynch: page 224
Phil Smith: pages 37, 45, 47, 53, 54, 59, 65, 68, 69, 71, 76, 77, 78
Press Association: pages 91, 94, 99, 212

Contents

Foreword

by Frankie Dettori

When Brough Scott first told me that he was putting together a compendium on me, based on the last thirty years or so as chronicled in the *Racing Post*, I imagined him locked in some dusty cellar under the office with strong coffee and a cold towel around his head!

When I went away and thought about a book with no involvement from myself other than this Foreword and the starring role, I really felt excited that I was the subject matter of something that would bring back great memories of the past thirty years, both good and bad.

The *Racing Post* has been there ever since I started so I guess we have grown together, and it is a huge honour that they have gathered enough to produce what I hope will be an interesting catalogue of my career and the events surrounding it.

Sometimes I feel that my life has been so busy that I have forgotten what really happened, so no doubt this will be as interesting for me as it will be for you the reader.

I'm not finished yet, so let's hope for a regular sequel!

Introduction

by Brough Scott

He is a shining star. He has risen and dipped and soared and crashed. He has been dragged from the wreckage and has been too close to the sun. He is both a party buzzer and a father-of-five family man. He is superbly skilful in the most perilous of sports. His heart can be on his sleeve or in his boots. He has lit up all around him like no man ever before. In 2015, with his future presumed in the past, Britain's favourite Italian has just delivered the greatest year of his riding life.

That's why we at *Racing Post* have put together this scrapbook of the story so far. For all of us it has been a fascinating process, particularly for me. Because it was a full forty years ago that I was writing about his father Gianfranco Dettori winning the Two Thousand Guineas at Newmarket, a feat repeated the next spring. When the young Frankie arrived here in 1975 I was already planning with Sheikh Mohammed the launch of *Racing Post*, which finally happened in April 1986. Frankie's first UK ride would not come for a twelvemonth but we logged it when it did. We have recorded everything since.

We have registered a lot else besides. By the nature of things our writers and photographers have been alongside him all the way. At first unwitting of how far it might go, then with by turns thrill, amazement, wonder, concern and even despair. Quite soon they realised that there was something very special in their midst. What none of us knew was quite how far, how high, how low or how long it would or could go on.

The fun of gathering this record has been its reminders of quite what an astonishing journey it has been. Of how much Frankie has achieved; of the terrible falls and professional crises, the mould-breaking technique and the barrier-busting effusiveness. Above all, from the process has emerged the sense of how lucky we are to have him.

Producing this record is not as easy as you might think, or we would hope it to be granted that we have all the words and pictures in our possession. In reality there is an enormous amount of drudgery wading through acres of print and folios of photos, and that is before the hiatus of 2000. For it was only in that year that *Racing Post* went digital, so there are now only limited photographic records from before that date, and the only access to words is through individual articles pasted into rows of stately red albums kindly stored at Weatherbys' headquarters in Wellingborough.

So it is to their James Schofield that our first thanks must go, but tribute must be paid to our own team led by Julian Brown and James Norris, who himself spent days in the Wellingborough archive. The digital delving deep into the *Racing Post* database was done by Andy Pennington, and the process of shifting copy and pictures onto the page was masterminded, as so successfully with our sister volume on AP McCoy, by the unmatchable 'book doctor'/designer duo of Sean Magee and John Schwartz – and all of us barked into line by the chummy smile and corgi snarl that is Liz Ampairee.

What we give you is not high on hindsight. Our guys have logged the snakes and ladders of the Dettori career as it was in front of them at the time. What has been selected is reproduced as it was then and, as a fellow toiler in the vineyard, I am rapt in admiration at their industry and erudition. For these pieces and photos were taken on the wing with occasionally a couple of days and more often only a few minutes to get them over before the increasingly desperate deadline-demanding phone calls started coming through.

But that is the beauty of it. This book is what it says on the tin. It is our record of how a little Italian came to cast the most visible footprint that his sport has ever seen. I hope you will see why we are proud to bring you this unique picture of a man who was, and amazingly remains, our brightest star.

EARLY YEARS

E veryone knows that Frankie Dettori is an Italian. Quite a few
are aware that he first came to England in his early teens to join
the Italian trainer Luca Cumani, and that his father Gianfranco
Dettori had been a champion jockey. But he arrived at Newmarket in
July 1985, and we did not launch the Racing Post until April 1986.
Even if we had wanted to, we were not around to record anything of the
childhood years. In September 2015, I went to Italy to put things right.

When Frankie Dettori arrived in Newmarket thirty years ago he
cried himself to sleep as a fourteen-year-old apprentice far from his
home in Milan. But there had been tears in Italy too. Even on his very
first ride at the famous San Siro racetrack when he was a tiny nine-
year-old and his mount was a little chestnut pony called Silvia. She
finished last, dumped him over her ears after the winning post and
someone shouted, 'You're nothing like your daddy!'

To understand what makes Dettori tick you need to go back to
his roots in the now faded grandeur of San Siro and its tattered old
training track not 5km from Milan's city centre. Once there you realise
why they called his father Il Monstro. It is Dettori's picture that is most
spotted on the walls of the Ribot restaurant. It is Gianfranco's hard,
gleaming, victory smile that is most synonymous with the glory days of
the 1970s and 1980s when he became thirteen-times champion jockey,
including a European record 229 winners in 1983. And all that despite
never having got on a horse until he was eighteen, and that only
because no-one else dared touch it.

Back here we revel in Frankie's story, but that of his father is in
many ways even more remarkable. Set for a life mixing concrete in
his native Sardinia, the teenage Gianfranco ran off to Rome to wash
dishes and work market stalls before getting better money mucking
out trotters and then Thoroughbreds at the racecourse. At eighteen
he begged for the chance to groom and ride a savage called Prince
Paddy. So well did the horse accept him that it was the unknown,
untried apprentice who was allowed to try him on the racetrack.
They won at the first time of asking and Gianfranco Dettori was on
his way.

In Britain we remember him as the short, powerful figure in the red and white hoops of top Italian owner Carlo d'Alessio who won the 1975 and 1976 Two Thousand Guineas with Bolkonski and Wollow for Henry Cecil.

As a two-year-old Bolkonski had been with d'Alessio's Italian trainer Sergio Cumani, whose son Luca was assistant to Cecil and who would later be so important for Dettori junior. It was Cumani senior who had taken Gianfranco to the top, but after Sergio's premature death it was to the training partnership of Alduino and Guiseppe Botti that the d'Alessio horses were transferred alongside their rider. Italian racing may have declined but team Botti most certainly has not. Last year Alduino's son Stefano, older brother of successful Newmarket trainer Marco, sent out no fewer than 260 winners from his modern base at Cenaia near Pisa, three hours south of Milan.

Near San Siro, there is not much that is modern at the Villa Bellotta, except Alduino's office. Time was when this Trenno Park training centre just up the road from the racetrack was teeming with Thoroughbreds. Now the grass grows long, the paint is peeling, and only a handful of two-year-olds file through the ancient courtyard before going out on what remains an oasis of green in the thickening urban sprawl of outer Milan.

But it suits Alduino, because it gives him quiet time with the young horses before passing them on to the training demands in Pisa. He has little room for more trophies as he sits behind his desk, a distinguished, grey, clipped figure in elegant dark-blue sweater and slacks. On the wall is a picture of him as an emaciated young jockey with the evocative headline: 'Il piccolo fantino prodigio' (the little jockey prodigy). Twice he was second to Frankie's father in the jockeys' championship. The wall has pictures of Gianfranco too.

Guiseppe Botti joins us. He was a successful steeplechase jockey until the pasta beat him, but not for nothing is the brothers' business partnership named Dioscuri after the mythical twins Castor and Pollux. Along with Guiseppe's two sons Endo and Alessandro, this is an awesome family unit.

They remember a much smaller family from forty years before. 'Gianfranco is one of the most determined, most professional men I have ever met,' says Alduino. 'He had never ridden until he was eighteen and he was always very, very dedicated to being the best. The crowd would shout "Bravo Monstro" when he came in on a winner. Frankie was in Gianfranco's shadow but he was always very lively, a tiny bit cocky, quite full of himself. Nothing,' concludes Alduino with something of an indulgent Don's smile, 'has changed much. But his father has been very, very important to him.'

The gifts that Frankie inherited did not only come from his father. Mara, his mother, was a juggler, contortionist, knife-throwing target, stand-up rider and trapeze artist in a flying circus. Her brother Claudio was the resident clown. She must have remained one of the few people profoundly unimpressed with the inadequacy of Frankie's flying dismount – 'Not even a somersault, darling?'

Gianfranco's courtship was as determined as his riding, and at sixteen Mara could not put up much resistance. Frankie and his older sister Sandra were permanent glories of the union but happiness was not, and by the time of Frankie's birth on 15 December 1970 the marriage was already doomed.

For all her circus glamour, Mara was a home bird, wholly unattracted to either fame or the racing game. Soon she and the two children were living on their own, but when Frankie was five it was decided that the kids would have a better start if they lived with their father and their new stepmother, Christine.

Financially it made sense, emotionally it sucked. 'The switch to living with my dad,' Frankie writes revealingly in his autobiography, 'was tough for me, even tougher for my sister, but toughest of all for Christine.'

He paints a stark picture of a strict and silent home where everything revolved around the 'grim and forbidding figure' of Dettori senior, whose punishments once stretched to making Sandra kneel bare-legged in a tray of salt. 'He was very wrong in the way he treated us as youngsters,' concludes Frankie before adding generously, 'but he didn't know any different, that's the way he was brought up too.' At fourteen Sandra ran back to her mother's, and Gianfranco, alarmed that he might also lose his son, bought Silvia, the chestnut pony on whom Frankie could fantasise that he could be a jockey like Daddy when he grew up.

The passion for Silvia did not last much longer than that abortive first experience at San Siro, and when she ran Frankie into a metal paddock rail, Dettori junior's ambitions were at least temporarily switched to the huge San Siro football stadium where AC Milan and Inter play on alternate Sundays and which rises like a modern monster opposite the old-fashioned racecourse across the road.

But the lure of the saddle was too strong, especially when his father took Frankie along to the major meetings. One afternoon Sheikh Mohammed's helicopter hovered down from the sky and out of it got the legend that is Lester Piggott. 'If you work hard, that could be you,' said Gianfranco. Within ten years it was.

The Botti brothers smile at their memories of the little mite who was allowed to leave school and work for them at the hardly senior

OPPOSITE: *Early days in Newmarket.*

age of thirteen and a half. But they accept that as Gianfranco's son he was always going to be in a rather privileged position and so applauded the idea of Frankie being explained the harsher facts of racing by Gianfranco's old sparring mate Tonino Verdicchio in Pisa.

From December to March Frankie tackled the basics – and how. On the first afternoon Tonino gave him a pitchfork, walked into the L-shaped, 24-box yard and said, 'I will start mucking out that end, you start this.' The diminutive Dettori's protest that at Botti's they only ever did three horses at a time was met with the unanswerable rejoinder, 'Well, there's no-one else here so you had better get on with it.'

The efforts, the experience and the warm Verdicchio family welcome worked so well that by the time Frankie returned to Milan he was getting very real ideas of being a jockey. Unfortunately he had also got himself a scooter, which he crashed and broke his right arm so badly that after three months it was still bent, and in Gianfranco's eyes extreme measures were called for. His son was loaded on to a normally quiet old horse called Fire Thatch that promptly ran away with him, and by the time it had pulled itself up the arm had straightened and the grand plan of dispatching Frankie to Luca Cumani in Newmarket could proceed on schedule.

Cumani remembers their first meeting. It had been in the paddock at Pisa when Gianfranco was riding for Cumani senior. 'Frankie was minute back then,' says Luca. 'He came in with his father who said, "When he's older I will send him to you." He eventually arrived in July 1985 but he was only fourteen and a half, didn't know anyone and didn't speak a word of English. I am sure he was homesick.'

Aldo Botti recalls Frankie coming up to him at the Newmarket sales that autumn, begging to be taken back to Milan. Yet a depiction even then of Britain's favourite Italian being all woe and tears on the pillow doesn't last long in conversation with Colin Rate, fellow Cumani apprentice, best mate and best man at the Dettori wedding.

'Frankie may have been a bit sad for the first few weeks when he didn't know anyone,' says Rate, whose strong Geordie tones are still traceable in some of Dettori's English-speak, 'but once he settled he

was always pretty cocky. We used to have a go at him for riding too short and there was a horse called Dallas who would whip round and drop him every time. We had a hell of a lot of fun but he was always mad for the riding.'

Rather too mad for Cumani when it was discovered that Dettori and Rate's idea of riding away the newly broken yearlings was to race them round the field pretending to be Steve Cauthen and Pat Eddery, then duelling for the jockeys' championship. 'Yes, he was quite a handful,' Cumani admits wryly, 'and back then he really wasn't that good a rider. He fell off a lot and you couldn't say he was any better than any other keen apprentice. But once he started race-riding you could see that he might become something special.'

In Britain apprentices cannot ride before their sixteenth birthday, but in Italy it is permitted from fifteen and a half, which in Frankie's case was 15 June 1986. Accordingly a three-ride trip to Italy was organised at the end of the month, which proved as hilarious as it was unsuccessful. The very first mount, on a filly called My Charlotte at San Siro on Wednesday 25 June finished as stone last as Silvia in that pony derby. The third ride saw Frankie get into a frantic, fifty-hit tangle with his whip, whacking himself as much as the luckless horse beneath him. The middle ride almost caused a riot.

Having Frankie's father, uncle and cousin in the eight-runner field was always asking for trouble and, with Frankie making the running while his father shouted instructions and wopped his son's horse over the tail, trouble is what they got. Mercifully Frankie's ride weakened in the closing stages and Gianfranco finally loosed the brake and won cosily. When Frankie returned that winter it was thought advisable to steer clear of Milan and too much family involvement.

So the first recorded winner of the Frankie Dettori riding career came in Turin on 16 November 1986 when a lop-eared old plodder called Rif slogged through the mud to notch his mark in history. From there the now winning jockey was dispatched to Naples, where the sauna was a dark cave heated by fires from the volcano and where Frankie's off-the-track education included a rather public loss of virginity in the back of a hooker's camper van.

But the racetrack was where it mattered, and he rode fifteen winners that winter. Among the jockeys was the experienced and skilful Bruce Raymond. 'You could see it straight away,' says Raymond. 'He had such balance and style. Everything you would want from someone of his age. When I got back to Newmarket I rang up my agent Matty Cowing and said, "You want to sign up that Dettori kid at Cumani's. He'll be champion for sure."'

Cowing would become Frankie's riding agent until his retirement in 1999. The appointment of Peter Burrell as business manager came not by outside recommendation but at Peter's own suggestion in the then smoky portals of Cuthie Suttle's betting shop. The young Dettori had been a ferocious punter to the extent of landing a massive coup when Richard Dunwoody and West Tip won the 1986 Grand National. He had backed the horse all winter down from 33-1 on the recommendation of Richard's father George, who rode out at Cumani's and on National afternoon Frankie left the betting shop with £1,900 in his tight little back pocket.

With great verve he bought himself a new scooter and his landlady a new washing machine before embarking on the inevitable process of giving the rest back to where it came from. 'Frankie was chalking the board when I came in,' says Burrell, then an assistant with Julie Cecil. 'I knew him because he was always shouting things when we passed each other in the strings. Back in the shop he told me he had punted all his money and as neither his father nor Luca would bail him out, he was having to work his debts off as a board man. He also said he would ride a winner next day. For some reason I said, "You are going to be champion and I will be your manager." We have been together ever since.'

You will see that by the time Il Monstro's son finally came to have his first ride in England at the end of April 1987 he was a long way from the nipper who burst into tears after going over Silvia's head at San Siro. After unsaddling 33-1 runner-up Mustakbil at Kempton, Frankie turned to the trainer, no less a figure than Derby-winning Peter Walwyn, pointed to the horse's heaving flanks and said, 'Not fit, too fat.'

Confidence was not going to be a problem, and if the first winner did not arrive until Goodwood on 9 June, it certainly came with suitable aplomb. The filly Lizzy Hare was named after Cumani's secretary who drove Frankie to the races, and was led up by Colin Rate, who had a flash new black suit with pink seams and matching shirt and socks in anticipation of the money he had on at 12-1. In the race Lizzy Hare was squeezed through a gap on the far rail to beat Dettori's idol Steve Cauthen by a stylish length and a half.

On the way home the winning jockey wrote 'Frankie goes to Hollywood' on a box of tissues. The road to the stars, and one or two trips to the depths, was under way. His Daddy would be proud of him.

In itself it had not been a race of much significance but in hindsight the report in the Racing Post *next day would have a huge impact. It would produce the first of more than a million words we have written about Frankie Dettori. The late, great George Ennor had the honour.*

Lanfranco Dettori got off the mark in Britain when landing the Birdless Grove Fillies' Handicap on Lizzy Hare.

The triumph of the young Italian, sixteen, was a welcome change of family fortune after his father broke a leg in two places in a Milan race on Saturday.

In a race in which five fillies were almost in line nearing the final furlong, Dettori got a lovely run up the inside rail to catch Interlacing (Steve Cauthen) well inside the last to win by a length and a half.

Dettori, whose father won the Two Thousand Guineas on Wollow and Bolkonski, joined Lizzy Hare's trainer Luca Cumani last year but was unable to be apprenticed then because he was too young.

Besides all the daily grind at the Cumani stables, including over-the-top celebrations when his mate Andy Keates led up Derby winner Kahyasi in 1988, there were technique-changing trips to California each winter. Based with Richard Cross at Santa Anita, Frankie was merely riding work on the first trip and only had a couple of race rides second time around. But he was amongst one of the greatest rosters of jockeys ever gathered together: Bill Shoemaker, Chris McCarron, Laffit Pincay, Gary Stevens and above all to Dettori, Angel Cordero.

In the long hours trudging rehab horses round the barns Frankie perfected imitations of his heroes in action, their low crouch, their pumping elbows, even the way they left the saddle. His tour de force *was the Angel Cordero 'flying dismount'. One day he would be confident enough to do it himself, but a lot of graft needed to go under the bridge beforehand. Eight winners were finally logged in 1987, another 22 in 1988, and by 1989 you could not fail to spot the American influence as the eighteen-year-old began to take the apprentice title by storm.*

In the month of June alone he racked up four trebles to his name. The first of them included a winner for the wife of Britain's greatest ever jockey, then unhappily detained at Highpoint Prison. After two years Frankie Dettori was back amongst the Racing Post *headlines, and he has never been far away from them since. Will O'Hanlon was the reporter.*

Frankie Dettori's budding talent shone through at overcast Leicester yesterday when the teenager completed his first hat-trick, at combined odds of 262-1, on Versailles Road, Follow The Drum and Ballyhooly.

Dettori had his claim reduced to three pounds after a fine win on Versailles Road (his first ride for the [Susan] Piggott stable) in the Allied Dunbar Handicap. He always had Versailles Road handily placed, took the six-year-old to the front from My Lamb early in the straight, and riding out with hands and heels, held off the renewed challenge of My Lamb in confident style by a length and a half …

Susan Piggott was full of praise for the eighteen-year-old son of Gianfranco, a long-time friend of the Piggott family and still going strong at the age of 48 – he rode the Italian Two Thousand Guineas winner Sikeston for John Dunlop earlier this year.

'That's Frankie's first ride for us but it won't be his last. He was excellent today,' Mrs Piggott said.

True to her word, Susan Piggott booked Frankie Dettori for Versailles Road in the Queen Anne Stakes at Royal Ascot and the young rider's bandwagon continued to roll at such a pace that by the time he won on

OPPOSITE: At Beverley, 1990.

Versailles Road again at Beverley in July he had lost all of his apprentice allowance. Being on level terms with his seniors never looked like stalling his progress, and a month later his career took a quantum leap when Luca Cumani promoted him to be stable jockey following Ray Cochrane's move to Guy Harwood.

Frankie had arrived – and, as Marcus Armytage wrote, he was aware of it.

Frankie Dettori was yesterday taking stock of the fact that, at the tender age of eighteen, he has landed one of the top jobs in British racing – stable jockey to the powerful Luca Cumani yard.

'I'm so pleased to have been given the job and the chance by Mr Cumani and the owners,' he said. 'I just hope I don't waste the opportunity.'

Dettori has not looked back since arriving at Cumani's Bedford House stables in Newmarket from Milan four years ago, when most English boys of his age were still at school.

'I was then working as a lad, with a kind of apprenticeship,' he explained. 'The following year I tried to get a licence, but at fifteen I was considered too young. During the winter I went back home, where you can ride at 15½. When we reapplied for a licence here at sixteen, I had already had sixteen winners in Italy, so I started with a 5lb claim instead of the usual 7lb.'

Dettori has matured his skills with the help of two trips to America in the last two winters, during which he has ridden out for Richard Cross in California. Last winter he had a couple of rides there, and he hopes to return in the close season.

He also has the right pedigree for such a high-powered job, although his desire to race-ride was not consciously inspired by his father Gianfranco's many and continued successes. Gianfranco rode the Two Thousand Guineas winner two years in succession for Henry Cecil, on Bolkonski and Wollow in 1975 and 1976.

'I was five at the time and wasn't old enough to be interested,' says the younger Dettori, who is now familiarly known by the anglicised version of his Italian name, Lanfranco.

'I was more intent on becoming a petrol pump attendant at that stage. As soon as I started to go racing, though, at the age of seven or eight, I knew that I wanted to be a jockey,' he said. It was at this stage that he was given his first pony, which gave him further encouragement.

'It's great having a father who also rides. He tells me all the secrets of the job,' Dettori added. 'But sometimes it can be hard for the sons of top jockeys to make it and that's partly why I came to Britain. When I wanted to start my father suggested that, as I was so young, I should go and learn in another country, see how I managed and then maybe go back home. He thought here would be better than France, and I've been here ever since.

'When I told my father about the new job he thought I was maybe a little young to take so much on. But you can't turn away such an opportunity as this, can you? Mr Cumani has been brilliant to me throughout. He's amazingly loyal to his jockeys and I'm really looking forward to next year.

'Up to now Markofdistinction is the best horse I've ridden, but I might have the chance of getting on some other top-class horses from now on.

'I'm very excited about the job, but a bit tired too. I couldn't sleep last night after I was told I was going to be number one.'

Dettori senior offered sage advice to his son:

'My advice would simply be to apply himself and carry on riding as he has done so far, and to continue to take things seriously. If he does that, he will be successful.

'Of course he will encounter problems, but only the usual ones that he might have gone through in the past. He will come through them in the same way as he always has.'

Problems would come but not in the short term. An injury to Ray Cochrane meant that good Cumani rides, including a first Classic mount in the St Leger, came sooner rather than later, as did a first Group race

*success and a final 75-winner total equalling the post-war apprentice
record set by Edward Hide in 1956.*

*Frankie's winter break included a belated passing of his driving test
and a first American winner, not to mention a ceremonial anointing
of private parts in hoof oil, at Hollywood Park, Los Angeles. Back in
England the bandwagon was swift to roll. In June he rode his first Royal
Ascot winner on Cumani's Markofdistinction. In August he became
the first teenager since Lester Piggott in 1955 to ride 100 winners in a
season , and to crown it all he rode Markofdistinction again to win the
Queen Elizabeth II Stakes at the Ascot Festival of Racing in September.*

Tim Richards reported on the Monday.

Champion apprentice, 1989.

Lanfranco Dettori's refreshing, youthful confidence shines through
like a beacon on the day racing encouraged everyone to join in the
festivities of its official Festival Day at Ascot on Saturday.

Shaking a clenched fist as he brought Markofdistinction back to
the winner's enclosure after the £206,000 Queen Elizabeth II Stakes,
he said: 'I've done it. My first Group 1 winner.'

Three quarters of an hour later nineteen-year-old Dettori
celebrated in the best possible way by going out and winning
his second Group 1 race, the Brent Walker Fillies' Mile, for
Markofdistinction's trainer Luca Cumani on Shamshir.

Dettori's feet had barely reached the ground as he dismounted
from Markofdistinction before he said: 'This must be the greatest day
of my life.'

He then walked straight into the arms of his proud father, former
Italian champion jockey Gianfranco.

Their joy was not to be concealed and they kissed not once, not
twice, but three times before walking arm in arm to the weighing
room.

Dettori, who this season became the first teenager to ride 100
winners in a season since Lester Piggott in 1955, had just outgunned
the champion Pat Eddery on Distant Relative in a gripping finish.

The confidence continued to bubble as the Italian boy climbed
onto a chair so he could address the press.

With Gianfranco after winning the Queen Elizabeth II Stakes, 1990.

'I have got nothing to say,' he said, pausing for the approving laughter.

But Dettori went on: 'My ambition was to ride 100 winners this season and win a Classic. For me, this today is very nearly a Classic and means a great deal.'

He added: 'My father was here when I won the Queen Anne Stakes on Markofdistinction at Royal Ascot and it is great that he could be here again for this.'

Dettori jumped off his chair, and ran back to prepare for victory on Shamshir, the Classic prospect bred by Cumani's Fittocks Stud.

He was last seen running to catch the seven o'clock flight from Heathrow to Canada, where he was due to ride Shellac at Woodbine yesterday. 'I won't need the plane – I'm flying already,' he quipped.

He will be back at Brighton tomorrow – in a hurry again on his way to reach for the stars.

The season ended with no fewer than 149 winners to finish fourth in the table, with only Pat Eddery, Steve Cauthen and Willie Carson ahead of him. The brief Californian trip logged six winners, including a $100,000 prize at Bay Meadows, but before Christmas the news had broken that the Aga Khan was removing all his horses, including 45 of Luca Cumani's, from Britain and that cast a shadow over the upcoming 1991 season that was never truly lifted.

The UK total for that year reached only 94 winners, though the highlights were a surprise victory in the German Derby, a Glorious Goodwood double for Luca Cumani, including Second Set in the Sussex Stakes, and an end-of-season approach to ride for Robert Sangster. A working trip to Hong Kong did little to cure the restlessness but gave Frankie the chance to experiment with the 'toe-in-the-iron' riding style advocated by his idol Angel Cordero.

At 101 winners, 1992 did at least produce a three-figure British total, highlighted in June with victory in the French Derby with Polytain and the Gold Cup at Royal Ascot with Drum Taps despite the toothy attentions of runner-up Arcadian Heights.

But the Cumani relationship was in trouble, and when Frankie went to the bright lights of Hong Kong again that winter, something had to give.

Robin Parke, our man in Hong Kong, broke the news.

Frankie Dettori has agreed terms to ride for Gary Ng Ting-Keung in Hong Kong.

It is understood Dettori has consented to a deal thought to be worth some £250,000 over two years. However, the contract hinges on two conditions.

The first involves Ng successfully applying for permission from the Royal Hong Kong Jockey Club to retain a stable jockey, while the second involves Dettori applying to the RHKJC for a jockey's licence.

Ng is prepared to retain Dettori and a verbal agreement has been reached.

However, it is understood there are reservations within the RHKJC about the precedent of the 22-year-old jockey riding in the colony under such circumstances. Philip Johnston, the director of racing, is on record as saying: 'We see Hong Kong as an important part of an individual jockey's career. We don't see it as a one-off situation.'

Should the move be sanctioned, Dettori will almost certainly have to sever his links with Luca Cumani.

It would have been rather better, to put it mildly, if Frankie had told Luca first. When he did get round to informing the trainer, he discovered that he no longer had a job in Newmarket. After a night out in London celebrating Arsenal's victory in the League Cup Final, he was not going to have a job in Hong Kong either. Robin Parke again:

Frankie Dettori's lucrative riding post in Hong Kong hung in the balance last night as local officials got wind of stories linking the jockey's name to a cocaine arrest in central London.

Local trainer Gary Ng Ting-Keung, who has agreed terms with Dettori for next season, vowed to stand by the jockey but his application to retain the rider depends on the verdict of the Royal Hong Kong Jockey Club Licensing Committee later this month.

'I've just spoken to Frankie on the phone and he has told me that everything is all right over there and that he is not in any trouble,' said Ng. 'I have applied to have him as my jockey next season and I will certainly stand behind him.

RHKJC officials were adopting a 'wait-and-see' policy yesterday. 'We will attempt to gather all the relevant information in relation to what we have heard,' explained Guy Watkins, RHKJC chief executive.

'Each case is treated on its merits and we will want the facts and anything relevant will be placed in front of the Licensing Committee when they meet on either 21 May or 24 May.'

Dettori, remanded on police bail after being arrested on suspicion of possessing drugs in London last month, was given a caution but not charged yesterday when he reappeared at Marylebone police station.

The jockey had been stopped by police near Oxford Street in London on 18 April, the day after he had ridden a high-profile four-timer at Newbury, including a winner for the Queen.

A police spokeswoman said: 'A 22-year-old man went back to Marylebone this morning and was given a police caution for being in possession of a controlled drug,' she explained. 'The substance involved was a small amount of cocaine.'

A police caution is effectively a warning, usually given for minor offences. However, the person involved must admit the offence and it goes on his police record.

The unwelcome publicity generated by the affair could not have come at a worse time for Dettori, just over a week before a meeting to decide whether he can take the job in Hong Kong.

The jockey was hoping yesterday that the whole affair would blow over as soon as possible. 'It wasn't me and the whole thing has been a big mix-up,' he said. 'Nobody could prove anything as I have done nothing wrong. I don't take drugs. I am not that stupid.

'I will admit to having a sleepless night as I knew there was a problem with the police but it did not concern me. I have done nothing wrong and I am in the clear.'

Dettori is currently serving out an eleven-day suspension but returns to action on Friday and is keen to get on with what he does best.

Sure enough, the door to Hong Kong was slammed shut, and the irony of this self-inflicted disaster is that it came the day after a four-timer at Newbury had looked as if the winning drought might finally be over. Yet the shame and the shock to the system proved the crucial course-correction for a young star otherwise heading for Hades.

He buckled down to such an extent that he had logged 149 winners by the end of the season. He had won a second Gold Cup on Drum Taps, and in Lochsong he had teamed up with the fastest horse of his career. He called her 'Linford Christie without the lunch box', and scorched home on her in the King George Stakes at Goodwood, the Nunthorpe at York and the Prix de l'Abbaye by an astonishing six lengths at Longchamp, after which he said:

Drum Taps wins his second Gold Cup at Royal Ascot, 1993.

'It was so exciting for me and I wanted to win by at least four lengths to clinch the sprint title. I've ridden many good horses but I've never been as fast as that in my life.'

By now Frankie was the subject of racecourse rumours once again, but this time they were positive. Michael Roberts was finding it impossible to hold down the job as first jockey to Sheikh Mohammed over more than a score of trainers around the country. Word had it that Frankie was to be hired to take over for the Sheikh's horses trained by John Gosden. Under instructions, the little Italian was uncharacteristically tight-lipped until rumours became fact in September.

'At least I won't have to keep walking around with a smile on my face and repeating that I know nothing! I have enjoyed riding for Mr Gosden this season and it seems to work very well. I am obviously

very keen to be champion jockey and I think riding for a stable such as Mr Gosden's will certainly help my chances …

'He has a big, strong team and well-bred horses, so it will be nice to ride for him. It is a very powerful stable and makes things easier for me as well.'

A year earlier Frankie had been in danger of throwing it all away. Now he had a second chance and, boy, didn't he take it.

TO THE STARS

T he intent positively screamed at us. The Frankie that showed up on New Year's Day on the Lingfield sand in 1994 was lean, tanned, shaven-headed – and silent. His father was with him and had told him, 'No big interviews,' and the son promptly won the first race and the third to let the riding do the talking.

So the Racing Post *report had only the briefest of Dettori comments. But it was obvious that something big could be around the corner.*

The 1994 Flat season starts today with no keener participant than Frankie Dettori, who this year starts his new job as No.1 jockey to Sheikh Mohammed and John Gosden.

Dettori, fresh from holiday in Morocco, was in double form on his return to action at Lingfield yesterday and is back at the track this afternoon for six rides and the chance of building a healthy lead over Pat Eddery when the turf season starts in March.

Sheikh Mohammed's new main jockey even intends a double stint next Saturday at Lingfield, followed by Wolverhampton's floodlight fixture in the evening.

Dettori said yesterday: 'I'm enjoying my work and would love to be champion. But it is a long season and I have to stay in one piece. Let's hope the year goes smoothly. I'm not really trying to get a head start on the other jockeys. When I walked into the weighing room today I thought it was March, all the boys are here – I want to ride from the beginning of the season to the end.'

He added: 'I feel fresh, fit and ready to go. I had a very relaxed holiday and was in bed by 9pm every night. Walking to the beach was the most exciting thing I did and I feel great for it.'

His all-weather campaign will be interrupted with trips to Dubai to ride for Sheikh Mohammed.

Pat Eddery is out to 11-8 from evens with the new jockeys' championship sponsor William Hill while Dettori is 7-4 from 9-4, having been 9-2 two weeks ago. Kevin Darley and Michael Roberts are 5-1 shots, followed by Richard Quinn at 16-1 and Willie Carson at 50-1.

Grand Lodge, left, touched off by Mister Baileys for the 1994 Two Thousand Guineas.

It didn't take long for those odds to change. Frankie rode his first treble on 7 January and had already kicked home 51 winners by the time the turf season started at Doncaster on 24 March.

There was a temporary setback at Newmarket's Guineas meeting with photo-finish defeats for both Balanchine in the One Thousand Guineas and Grand Lodge in the Two Thousand, but at a rain-soaked Epsom it all came good again as Frankie drove Balanchine up the stands rail to win the Oaks. It was Sheikh Mohammed's first big dividend from wintering his horses in Dubai, and a first Classic for his jockey.

Tim Richards reported:

Dettori, touched off in both Guineas, gave a salute and a yell of delight as he pulled up. 'That was for my parents, who have been so supportive,' he said.

'After getting beaten in photos for both the Two Thousand and One Thousand Guineas I was feeling just a little bit sour. I thought at least one of them would have gone my way, but this makes up for everything.

'I spoke to Dad and John Gosden this morning about how I should ride the race and they said be positive. There will always be room for her in my heart as my first Classic winner in England.'

'I thought that I should be handy on her but with a lead I let her slip into second going down the hill, and when I went for home she

Balanchine sluices home in the Oaks, 1994.

just kept on galloping. After I'd been beaten in the two Guineas I was afraid that something would come up and do me and I kept shouting for the post to come.'

Fortune was smiling in every way. In the week after the Derby Frankie not only got the 100 up for the season, but found forgiveness from both overseas and much closer to home. This from Graham Green.

Frankie Dettori is to team up with Luca Cumani for the first time in more than eighteen months after being booked yesterday to ride Relatively Special in the Coronation Stakes at Royal Ascot next week.

Cumani, Dettori's mentor from the day he left Italy to pursue a riding career in Britain, has not employed the jockey since he partnered Inner City to win a Group 3 race at San Siro, Italy on 8 November 1992.

Dettori severed his eight-year association with Cumani's Bedford House yard in February last year having decided to take up a lucrative retainer in Hong Kong. His decision resulted in Cumani making alternative riding arrangements.

Ironically, Dettori's Hong Kong stint was eventually blocked by the Hong Kong Jockey Club although the jockey has now been granted a three-month contract with the colony this winter.

Frankie was hot property, but not as hot as Lochsong, the lightning-fast sprinter who took the breath away in the King's Stand Stakes. An excited Frankie told the press:

'She's not a racehorse. She's more than that, a machine. A powerhouse. It's like driving a high-powered car in top gear all the way.

'She's a once-in-a-lifetime ride and I think every bit as good as Dayjur. I don't think we'll get to see another horse like this in our lifetime. If we do I'd like to ride it.'

Fillies were breaking new ground for Frankie, and at the end of June 1994 Balanchine took him and Sheikh Mohammed to new heights by beating the colts in the Irish Derby. Tony O'Hehir reported from County Kildare:

Sheikh Mohammed's Dubai experiment reached new heights when Balanchine trounced the colts in the Budweiser Irish Derby at the Curragh yesterday.

The Energizer Oaks winner, a 5-1 chance, powered home four and a half lengths clear of the even-money favourite King's Theatre with

'A machine' – Lochsong wins the King's Stand Stakes.

Colonel Collins (11-2) three and a half lengths away in third. Alfriffa was fourth.

Balanchine was completing the same double achieved by Salsabil in 1990, and her win was a resounding vindication of the Maktoums' decision to winter her and other horses in Dubai.

A delighted Sheikh Mohammed, whose Godolphin operation owns Balanchine in partnership with his brother Maktoum al Maktoum, was one of the first on the track to greet the winner. Grabbing Frankie Dettori (for whom Balanchine was a first Irish Classic winner) by the hand, Sheikh Mohammed led the Derby heroine back.

Whatever disappointment he may have felt over King's Theatre's defeat was more than compensated for by Balanchine's achievement.

Commenting on the decision to supplement Balanchine to yesterday's race, at a cost of Ir£60,000, Sheikh Mohammed said: 'The whole thing is about sport. They must race against each other to see who is better.'

Sheikh Mohammed indicated that Balanchine is likely to miss the King George VI and Queen Elizabeth Diamond Stakes. He said: 'The King George comes in the middle of the season and if you run there you may not have your horse right to run in the Arc.'

Dettori, who clapped his hands above his head before dismounting, to the delight of the crowd, said: 'She is great. After three furlongs she started pulling. Three furlongs out, I said 'Come on, let's go and win the race.'

'I knew at the furlong pole it would take a machine to pass us, we were going so fast.

'She has won two Classics and been beaten a short head in a third. No words can describe her, she was unbelievable – much better than at Epsom. She flew from the three-furlong marker and spread them out like eagles, absolutely tremendous.'

That first day at Lingfield already seemed an age away but the winners kept coming and by 2 September an almost unthinkable 200 was up. Ray Gilpin was our man in the north.

Frankie Dettori may delay his departure to Hong Kong this winter in a bid to beat Sir Gordon Richards' all-time record of 269 winners in a single season after completing his first double century at York yesterday.

Dettori – only the sixth jockey in history to reach this landmark and just the fourth this century – reached the 200-winner mark in style via a 67-1 treble on the Knavesmire on Lower Egypt, Menas Gold and Shoaq Albarr.

And, having achieved the double century a full seven weeks earlier than Michael Roberts and Pat Eddery, the 23-year-old immediately started to think of new targets.

The first on his agenda is topping the 227 winners partnered by his father Gianfranco in Italy in 1983. Beyond that comes Richards' record score, achieved in 1947 – and Dettori admitted yesterday he might not be able to resist a crack.

Dettori's 200 has been achieved much earlier than those of Roberts and Eddery, the legacy of a season which saw him in winning action from the very first: he scored aboard the Neil Graham-trained Tiddy Oggie in the San Sebastian Median Auction Stakes, which started at 12.45pm on New Year's Day at Lingfield.

'I did not want anyone to get a start on me so I began on the all-weather; and I can tell you boys that it was a hard old winter and very cold but I worked very hard and it paid off,' he said.

It took Roberts until 21 October to ride his 200th winner two years ago, while Eddery achieved the feat two days later in 1990.

But this season belongs to Dettori as he has ploughed through an astronomical 1,057 rides to achieve his goal.

And there was no disguising his delight as he dismounted from the John Gosden-trained Shoaq Albarr. 'I've done it at last,' he beamed. 'I didn't realise how hard it was going to be but it's all paid off in the end.'

Dettori received a great reception from the crowd as he rode into the winner's enclosure. 'It is great to do it here and on one of the guv'nor's horses,' he said. 'My fiftieth and one hundredth winners this season were also for him and I did not expect to get to 200 so soon.'

Gosden paid tribute to his man. 'Frankie has many qualities and his sheer love of racing is a pleasure to see,' he said. 'He has superb hands, very good judgement and great balance, and he always gets the most out of his horses before going for his whip.'

The Gordon Richards total of 269 winners for the 1947 season was to prove out of reach, but Frankie's final score of 233 had the filial satisfaction of edging ahead of his father's Italian record.

It left him tired but still motivated as he talked to Rodney Masters before jetting to Kentucky for the Breeders' Cup. He had Barathea for Sheikh Mohammed and Luca Cumani in the Mile and Lochsong in the Sprint. But those were not his only ambitions.

Frankie Dettori lifts off today for Louisville and takes in five million dollars-worth of Breeders' Cup action with a surprise up his sleeve.

Many regarded his wickedly fatiguing, but ultimately triumphant, champion jockey challenge as a one-off project for 1994.

This year, his first retained by Sheikh Mohammed, was smash and grab before the rest knew what was happening, foot hard down on the power pedal and spraying up all-weather sand from New Year's Day.

A skilfully devised and superbly executed one-off had indeed been the original conception, but, as the award-winning actor found, the first Oscar inspires harder graft to secure a second.

Dettori's surprise package comes in his privately pledged decree of intent. He has, according to close friends, passionately set his heart on collecting at least nine more championship titles, an ambition motivated by his desire to mirror a statistic logged on Italy's racing records. His father, Gianfranco, was ten times champion jockey.

The last jockey to string together successive titles stretching to double figures was Gordon Richard more than forty years ago.

'The championship means more to Frankie than initially he thought it would, and he'll go to any lengths to retain it year after year,' says Bruce Raymond, one of the first to identify the youngster as a future world-class talent, watching him ride as a fifteen-year-old in Naples, and later fixing him up with agent Mattie Cowing.

'If next year Jason Weaver or Pat Eddery get too close, Frankie will simply step up the tempo and work harder to see them off,' adds Raymond. 'It's important for his personality to be No.1, it expands the attention he adores and thrives on.'

'And now he's at the top, I'm sure that he'll let his natural exuberance spill over even more. We saw an indication of that when he planted a kiss on Ian Balding after Lochsong's win in Paris. Could you imagine John Matthias doing that after winning on Glint Of Gold? Somehow Frankie gets away with it; his endearing charisma overwhelms and engulfs all in its path.

'His public image is the real thing, his only image. There's no other Frankie. You will never find a jockey to say a bad word about him, and most are trying now to ride like him, toes in the irons. He is inspiring generations old and new.'

His bewitching smile has alone broken down sporting barriers, putting him up there with the non-racing public on a level with Lester Piggott and Desert Orchid. A smile sufficiently wide to bridge the Atlantic and win over America too.

They remember him in the offices of Enterprise Rent-A-Car in Los Angeles, where he arrived before last year's Breeders' Cup, fitted out with wrap-around £120 Camel dark glasses, top-of-the-range Armani suit, and requesting a fast and flashy motor – a Lexus Sports convertible. He had staff in meltdown.

'We thought he was an Italian film star over to do a movie in Hollywood. His personality was giving off sparks like a firework, he captivated us all,' says the office manageress. 'When he wrote "jockey" on the leasing form we thought he was kidding us, and maybe it was a trick to avoid publicity. He could make it big out here.'

However, his smile lines channelled a few tears when Dettori's anchors lost rip, his world drifting in dangerous waters. Difficult times when, potentially, he could have been a star recruit for the brat pack.

London drugs police felt his collar and cautioned him and, after the well-chronicled ruck over ambitions to make it rich quick in Hong Kong, he was sacked by Luca Cumani who, apart from family, he respects most. He also had a very public argument with a journalist outside the Newmarket weighing room.

Dettori took a Cumani boot up the backside hard enough to fly him to the top row seats of the Colosseum. The overall experience is said to have scared him.

'He took some knocks and the threat of facing an uncertain future shook him into growing up,' says Cumani. 'It made him realise what life is all about. His behaviour had been babyish. Now his attitude is completely professional and our relationship is on the rails again. He's back where his talent demands he should be.'

Two of his four rides on Saturday will be on Cumani-trained horses, Only Royale and Barathea. His other mounts are Paul Kelleway's Belle Genius and, of course, Lochsong, who will need all Dettori's sweet whispering to keep her cool in the fizzing cauldron that is all part of Churchill Downs. A world away from a sedate Sunday at Longchamp.

Apart from Cumani, other influences to steady the Dettori career wobble were his father, who now spends more time in Newmarket, and agent Mattie Cowing who, at 57, is more than twice his client's age.

His youth shields against burn-out after 1,300-plus home mounts, but flames are licking at the edges. 'He's getting tired now, that's for sure,' says Cowing. 'But he has seen it out tremendously well. I'm sure many others would have fallen by the wayside under such a demanding schedule.

'His attitude has been professional throughout. Whatever weight he was requested to do, he did. He doesn't put me under pressure, although he might occasionally ask, "Why didn't I ride this horse?" I'll explain and he'll accept it without further debate.

'Riding his first British Classic winner on Balanchine in the Oaks was of the utmost importance to him after getting beaten by short heads in both the Two Thousand and One Thousand Guineas. It would be a close call what means most to him, that Classic or the championship.'

Taking virtually all of December off, probably spending two weeks at his father's villa or on a beach in Morocco, as he did over the same time last year, he has instructed Cowing to programme the all-weather assault from 1 January.

The game is changing next year, however, with both Eddery and Weaver playing under different rules, freelancing for the first time. Dettori and Cowing fear most the man they dethroned, and feel they must get first run again.

'I'm sure Pat will be a danger to us,' predicts Cowing. 'His movements will not be restricted by the [Khalid] Abdullah contract, he'll ride what he wants. It's a strong positon.'

When, and if, Dettori stacks his ten championships, what then? Perhaps some will get their wish and the movie-makers will make sure Frankie goes to Hollywood.

At Churchill Downs Lochsong could not handle the pressure, but Barathea could. The filly used up all her juice running away in an on-track training gallop but Barathea was the very sweetest of

Delirious delight as Barathea wins the Breeders' Cup Mile at Churchill Downs in 1994.

recompense. And the perfect reunion for Frankie and Luca Cumani, his original mentor.

And it was to give us the first showing of what was to become Frankie's post-race trademark – the Flying Dismount.

The pride and joy went shamelessly undisguised. Barathea's record-breaking victory in the Breeders' Cup Mile reduced his trainer Luca Cumani and seasoned head lad Ian Willows to tears, while Frankie Dettori could not stop punching the Kentucky skies.

Witnessing one of those famous moments in sport, I was sandwiched between Willows and Barathea's lad Keith Leddington and, in ecstatic scenes as their hero flashed past the post, was all but launched over the rails onto the dirt track.

Leddington lifted owner-breeder Gerald Leigh and whirled him in a victory dance. Dettori kissed Cumani, who stood there in tears amid a sea of congratulations.

Dettori could not contain himself and, dismounting, did an Angel Cordero leap from the saddle, throwing himself skywards, arms stretched, before landing on the ground.

'Angel is my idol and I did the Cordero leap,' said Dettori. 'Mr Cumani and I said that if we won a big one in the States I would do a Cordero leap – and I did.'

Dettori summed up the feelings of the British contingent when he said: 'It is very important for British racing as well as myself that we can come over here and do this.

'Winning Classics is great at home but the build-up to this through the week has been fantastic. And, after that build-up, I released all the tension as I passed the post.'

Frankie began 1995 true to his word, starting in the first week of January and immediately logging up seven winners in three days. Saeed bin Suroor was the new Godolphin trainer and Frankie duly won the French Two Thousand Guineas for them on Vettori and the Oaks at Epsom on Moonshell. A week after Epsom the 100 was up for the season a week after.

Not everything went right. He rode Gosden's Tamure to finish second to Godolphin's Lammtarra in the Derby, and Red Bishop rather than the winner Halling in the Eclipse. But a call-up to ride Lammtarra in the King George VI and Queen Elizabeth Diamond Stakes at Ascot had a headline afterwards of 'Frankie Jumps for Joy', and Tim Richards had a happy jockey to talk to.

Lammtarra once again defied his inexperience and wrote another glorious chapter in a remarkable story in winning a thrilling King George VI and Queen Elizabeth Diamond Stakes at Ascot on Saturday.

He has now added the Derby and King George to his Listed-race success at two – an amazing achievement for a horse who

Lammtarra battles home to beat Pentire in the 1995 King George.

Royal recognition after the 1995 King George.

was taken seriously ill in Dubai over the winter and then had to overcome a training setback which meant he missed the Irish Derby.

Running for only the third time, Lammtarra's never-say-die attitude shone through as he became the tenth Epsom hero to go on to Ascot glory in the last 25 years.

And if the blue-blooded son of Nijinksy and Snow Bride enjoys a trouble-free run up to the Arc, there is no telling what he may achieve in Europe's autumn championship.

Ascot's mid-summer championship is safely in the bag, but only after an epic battle with Pentire.

Lammtarra, under a fine ride from Walter Swinburn's replacement Frankie Dettori, forged a neck up on Pentire to the finish to provide a good result for the three-year-olds and a much-needed boost for the Derby form, and basking in the glory of his great victory on Saturday, Dettori was quick to reveal the part played by Swinburn. 'I spoke to Walter on Friday,' he said. 'He was very nice about it and he helped me a lot. If it wasn't for him, perhaps I would have got beat today.'

'The thing Walter was scared of was the short straight and the fact that there might not be much pace. He said, "Be bold with him and dig deep because he will find more."'

Dettori went on: 'Being drawn on the outside, I was able to control my rhythm without checking too much. In the straight when Pentire came to me, he was looking very good. But the further we were going the further my horse was going to go away. Perhaps with a longer straight we would have won more comfortably.

'There were a lot of doubts about Lammtarra but he showed himself to be a true champion.'

Describing the feeling as he passed the post with a whip salute to the cheering crowd, Dettori said: 'It sent shivers up my spine – probably one of the best moments of my life.

'A lot of great horses have won the King George, horses like Ribot. For me it's one of the most important races – this, the Arc and the Derby. And it's a great thrill to win any of them.'

Spills as well as thrills are an ever-present threat to a jockey and in early August Frankie got a real knockout of a fall when an old horse called Wainwright snapped his leg at full gallop at Haydock.

Getting back for York was touch and go, but So Factual made it worth it by skating up in the Nunthorpe. It was another big day for Godolphin but not as big for either training operation or for jockey as when Classic Cliché gave them the St Leger and Frankie his 1,000th winner at only 24. Tim Richards reports:

Returning on So Factual at York.

The king is dead, long live the king. It was as if Frankie Dettori knew that he had taken over the mantle of racing's greatest asset from Lester Piggott at Doncaster on Saturday.

As Piggott's successor, Dettori could not be more different.

For the bubbling Italian, the back-slapping was incredibly almost one way. He wanted to share the joy of his 1,000th British victory on Classic Cliché in the Pertemps St Leger with everyone at Doncaster as well as the millions of television viewers.

His infectious enthusiasm spilled out across Town Moor and, courtesy of the TV cameras, into the pubs, clubs and sitting rooms throughout the country.

Delighted Dettori was punching shoulders, slapping backs and shaking hands as if it was everyone else who should be congratulated.

He loves the world to be part of *his* occasion and would hate them to forget it. If you hadn't been paying attention, you soon were.

A hearty crack on the shoulder as he walked towards you or a pat on the back as he came up behind you. He wanted to talk to everyone. 'Wasn't it great?' was the opening gambit as he signed autographs for young and old. Of course, they agreed.

An elderly couple strolling in the autumn evening sunshine of a Yorkshire village had enjoyed the Dettori show on television. Non-betting, their interest in racing had always been from a distance. But on Saturday they became part of it.

'Frankie is lovely and fresh, the way he comes over. He obviously loves what he's doing, which isn't always the impression you get from top sportsmen. You can't help liking him even though you haven't met him,' they agreed.

Even after taking on the role of the Grand Prix-winning driver and showering the photographers with champagne, Dettori leapt in amongst them to show no ill feeling. The paparazzi were left smiling.

Dettori, whose first winner in England was Lizzy Hare at Goodwood in June 1987, said: I feel on top of the world; I can't believe I reached my 1,000 so quickly. It seems like I started yesterday. The time has gone so quick and I hope the next twenty years don't go so fast because I want to enjoy them even more.'

The son of former Italian champion jockey Gianfranco Dettori, Frankie won his first race in Italy when he was fifteen. 'I remember it well,' he said with a smile. 'The horse was a nine-year-old and won a seller in Turin.'

Dettori, on 177 wins for the season after a dashing double, was anxious to pay tribute to the people who helped him up the ladder of fame.

'Luca Cumani, Sheikh Mohammed, my great new boss John Gosden who is like a father figure to me, and Ian Balding, Lord Huntingdon and David Loder have all supported me through the years,' he enthused. 'Now I want to try and ride 300 winners this season.'

The cheers of the crowd, aware that the Dettori factor had made Classic Cliché 100-30 favourite, were testimony to his popularity.

He responded by raising his arms aloft and even threw his goggles into the mass of converging racegoers as he returned to unsaddle. The now celebrated Angel Cordero-style leap from the saddle was greeted with further acclaim.

He loved the attention. So did we. And so should racing.

Frankie's achievements were now being measured against the greatest in the game. That means winning the greatest of prizes. In October 1995 it was to be the Arc on Lammtarra. Colin Russell was among the throng.

Frankie Dettori has probably never been seen in a more determined light than when driving Lammtarra to victory in yesterday's Prix de l'Arc de Triomphe.

He has never lacked confidence, in either the horse's ability or his own, so it was no surprise that he rode a positive race, seeing daylight throughout, not risking the bashing and buffeting that can ruin an Arc chance, particularly that of a horse whose racing experience was limited to only three runs.

Always handy behind the pace-setting Luso, Dettori kicked him into the lead two and a half furlongs out.

When he splayed his arms sideways, changing the reins in his hands in a style that has become his trademark, we knew the rest of his lines by heart.

Body crouched, hands driving forwards, more rein-changing, a few taps with the whip and head down to the line. A proven formula.

But yesterday was different. After the initial movement of reins, he still had a fight on his hands. More was needed and more was given.

The whip came out for a time just under two furlongs from home when Dettori gave the horse two good taps on the right, before changing hands.

Uninhibited joy from Frankie as Lammtarra lands the 1995 Arc.

In an ordinary race, under the watchful eye of the British stewards with Jockey Club Instruction H9 as their guideline, further use of the stick would have been sparing.

Not so at Longchamp in the Arc; two more good cracks were given and Lammtarra responded. But he still needed more and this was when we witnessed Dettori as we had never seen him before.

A crack, a stride or two more, another crack, then another, and another – about fifteen times in all. Lammtarra answered him, and continued to do so.

It was hard work, not pretty, but a jockey doing what he was paid to do, win a race. Maybe the odd one was over shoulder height, but his horse battled, the punters cheered, Lammtarra won the Arc.

Had it been Ascot or Epsom, a visit to the stewards' room would have been obligatory, not for congratulations, but for an explanation about his use of the whip.

'He responded, he won,' would not have been good enough and the jockey could have expected a lengthy ban. But missing the Champion Stakes and the heady delights of Yarmouth and Folkestone somehow would have paled into insignificance.

Dettori won the Arc. He did not do it in his usual way, but he did it.

The French press can be pretty hard to please. Not this time:

Frankie Dettori was heralded by the French press as the new king of Longchamp after a scintillating victory on Lammtarra in Sunday's Arc.

Le Figaro described Dettori as 'inspiration … having achieved the impossible by becoming king of Longchamp straight away – it took years for Lester Piggott and Cash Asmussen to accomplish the same feat.'

The overall praise centred on the 24-year-old's apparent ability to ride equally well on racecourses all over the world.

Paris-Turf, France's only daily racing newspaper, summed up Dettori's unique talent. 'He is not only very gifted at race-riding but he is also extremely likeable and intelligent,' it said.

'His numerous travels have given him an important knowledge of the racing world and whether the racing be in Japan, England, Italy or France, it holds no secrets for him.'

Le Parisien focused on Dettori's crowd-pleasing ability, detailing how the Italian 'livened up the afternoon … by playing the jester'.

It added: 'He blew kisses to the sky and to the Maktoum family, he sprang off his horse and he raced along the stands rail waving his trophy in the air.'

Wedding bells: Frankie and Catherine tie the knot in 1997.

A day after Paris, Frankie was in trouble with the Stewards at Pontefract but 24 hours later he was the toast of York with a treble that took him to 200 for the season.

Big things beckoned in 1996, not least his Valentine's Day engagement to the lovely university student Catherine Allen, whom he had first met eighteen months earlier as she led him round on a horse he was to ride in the last at Haydock.

He won the Two Thousand Guineas on Mark Of Esteem for Godolphin in a three-way photo so intense that all three jockeys got whip suspensions. He was third in the Derby on Shantou, and rode six winners on the next Friday, only to shatter his elbow when a filly flipped over with him in the paddock at Newbury a day later.

It was a bad break and he was not back with us until August. When he was, we realised what we had been missing when Halling won the Juddmonte at York and then Mark Of Esteem duly bolted up in the Celebration Mile at Goodwood. But from a partnership point of view not much was going to beat Shantou's victory in the St Leger. A fifth Classic for Frankie but a long overdue first for his saviour, John Gosden. That significance was not overlooked by Paul Haigh.

Don't think about Sunday just yet. The St Leger may not have very much bearing on any of the great events over the next six weeks, although it did provide a window of opportunity for some of us to gaze wistfully at the fantasy that here was a vindication of the Derby form. (At least for the quarter of an hour or so before the amazing Timarida slammed that window shut).

But the Leger was too good to forget. The old race must be safe now for a while from those who've questioned its usefulness, who think it should be opened up to all-comers, like its French and Irish counterparts. There's no need for that sort of talk while the venerable Classic serves up battles like this.

Whose triumph was it?

The horses? Well, ye-es. It's always got to be the horses, hasn't it? But Saturday's two equine principals are both, one suspects, slightly dodgy characters: neither of them of startling ability if judged by the highest standards; neither of them completely besotted with the idea of racing as a way of earning their keep.

This not an accusation you can level at the humans involved: at Pat Eddery or Henry Cecil, at Frankie Dettori… or John Gosden.

At first glance you have to say it was Frankie's day. When Dushyantor strolled into the lead, only a fool, or someone who hadn't seen the Derby, would have guessed that Shantou could possibly come and do him this time. Not when he'd had a clear run without the irritation of undulations or any of the other things that put him off his stride at Epsom.

If anything was going to come from the back and give the favourite a race, you'd have said two out it was going to be St Mawes. But then you saw Frankie winding Shantou up. You saw that Frankie had made up his mind to win. You saw the horse wasn't going to be given the option to refuse.

There is certainly no better jockey riding in Europe now than our reigning champion. Maybe there's no better jockey in the world. There may be one or two who've got a clear, rather than a fuzzy, memory of Piggott at the same age who'll say this is going over the top, but here's one observer who's not absolutely sure he's ever seen anyone riding better than Frankie is at the moment.

Celebrating St Leger victory on Shantou in 1996.

Another winner for John Gosden, mentor and friend.

It won't be long before someone starts calling him a genius, which he's not of course. Or at least he's not just because he can ride like he does. He's just a man with an extraordinary knack for making horses run to the very best of their ability. Which isn't quite the same as genius, is it? It doesn't half make good watching, though – even when you haven't got a penny on.

Pat was good on Saturday. Frankie was brilliant, and he knew it. Didn't you see it in his face? Just after he passed the post? That was about as good as it gets – whatever the Jockey Club says.

But it wasn't really Frankie's day – and that remark has nothing to do with the truly absurd, almost disgraceful, decision to penalise the pair of them for supposedly 'excessive' use of the whip. Frankie has too many days to need another day anyway. The man who'll derive most contentment from Saturday will be Shantou's trainer, whose first English Classic success this was.

John Gosden's had a long wait, too long for some of those who've assumed that, as the supposed recipient of the pick of Sheikh Mohammed's horses, he should be mopping up great races like gravy off a plate.

In fact Gosden doesn't get all the cream and never has done. Over the last couple of years he's lost some to Godolphin – not least

Halling, a horse you can either say he prepared for what he's become, or, if you want to be unfair, you can say possessed a potential Gosden failed to maximise. The failure to send out a Classic winner has been cited as some proof that Gosden hasn't quite got what it takes.

Well that's over now. The dam's been broken. John Gosden is a very good trainer as well as an excellent man.

Got that?

Good. Now you can think about yesterday and all that day's events have told us.

Victory had come at a cost for Frankie's finishing efforts earned him another suspension and so gave him an odd slice of history by becoming the first jockey to collect separate whip bans for winning two Classics in the same season.

Within the month, Frankie would be making history of a much wider kind.

THE MAGNIFICENT SEVEN

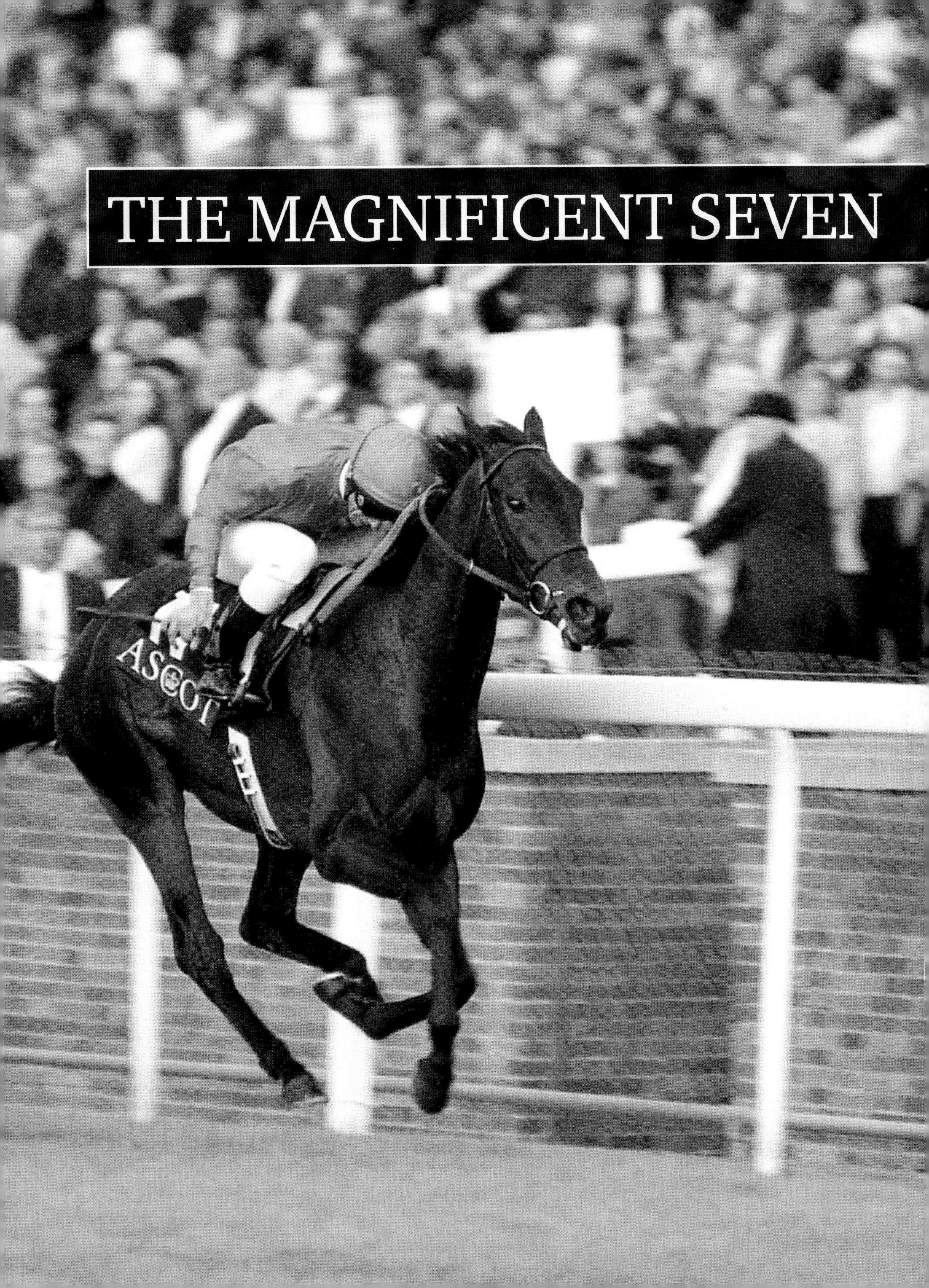

The greatest riding feat in racing history was preceded by something of a Dettori winner-drought. It was only on Friday 27 September 1996 that he returned from a four-day whip suspension from that driving finish in the St Leger, and the comeback was anything but a success – six losers and a long drive back down the M6 from Haydock.

Saturday 28 September 1996 was to be rather better.

Beforehand the prospects of a successful day looked good, but not that good. The main set-up piece in the Racing Post *did include the words 'The Magnificent Seven', but that was only in the context of the seven runners in the Queen Elizabeth II Stakes, and the only single reference to Frankie was as the rider of Two Thousand Guineas winner Mark Of Esteem. By next morning things were rather different. 'Dettori' and 'Magnificent Seven' were etched together into the legend of the game. Nick Godfrey put it on the record.*

Frankie Dettori made history yesterday when he achieved the seemingly impossible by riding all seven winners on the first day of Ascot's Festival meeting.

A magical afternoon saw the champion return to a tumultuous reception after completing the 25,095-1 seven-timer which rates as one of the greatest riding achievements of all time.

Dettori, his characteristic grin wider than ever, was well aware of its significance as he returned on Fujiyama Crest, the final winner of a day in which Mark Of Esteem provided the highlight with his devastating win in the Queen Elizabeth II Stakes.

'Is there any more racing for me? – I'm just warming up!' quipped the 25-year-old. 'It's everybody's dream to ride a few nice winners at Ascot and it's everybody's dream to go through the card.

'I always felt that perhaps one day I could do it – but I can't believe I've done it at such a competitive meeting.

'I've had some great days in my life but this takes all the beating. One thing's for sure, I'm definitely going to do the Lottery tonight!'

Whisked away to a balcony to be interviewed by the BBC, Dettori waved to the cheering crowd, shouted 'I love you!' and flung his goggles into the throng of thrilled and smiling faces.

Dettori started out with the first of four winners for Godolphin on 2-1 shot Wall Street in the Cumberland Lodge Stakes. Two more Pattern victories followed on Diffident (12-1) and Mark Of Esteem (100-30) before Decorated Hero (7-1), Fatefully (7-4), Lochangel (5-4) and Fujiyama Crest (2-1) completed an amazing afternoon's work.

He is the first jockey to ride seven winners on one card in Britain and bookmakers estimate that his efforts cost them millions. Certainly it affected the price of Fujiyama Crest as Dettori went out for his epoch-making ride.

'I saw he was 12-1 in the paper and I was a bit surprised he went off at 2-1,' said Dettori. 'I'm sure everybody had a pound on him.

'God was on my side,' he added. 'After I'd won six I thought it would be impossible to win seven.

'In the seventh race I couldn't believe I could win, so I just let it all go and floated to the front and if he kept going, great, but if not, it had been a great day. And he won.'

Dettori was cheered to the echo as he returned to the winner's enclosure on Fujiyama Crest.

One! Wall Street wins the opening Cumberland Lodge Stakes.

He performed his second flying dismount of the day after one to celebrate Mark Of Esteem's victory.

Ironically, the Ascot stewards had earlier asked him to contain his enthusiasm. 'We asked him not to jump off for safety reasons,' said stewards' secretary Patrick Hibbert-Foy.

'Some of us are of the opinion that it could be dangerous, but there is nothing against it in the rules.'

Dettori himself was going to refrain from the flying dismount on Mark Of Esteem until owner Sheikh Maktoum stepped in. 'He looked at me to ask me if I was going to do it,' said the Italian.

Two! Diffident, near side, edges out Lucayan Prince (black and white colours).

'It's his horse, and I obliged him with what he wanted. Mark Of Esteem is a lovely horse and I'm sure he didn't mind.'

The late George Ennor was our senior reporter. He had been around the block more times than Perseus. But he had never seen anything like this.

I have been lucky enough to witness many amazing achievements during my 38-plus years in racing, but to have been at Ascot yesterday to see Frankie Dettori ride those seven winners was something I shall never forget.

It was truly one of those 'I was there' occasions, on a par with Red Rum's third Grand National, Sea-Bird winning the Derby and the Arc, Desert Orchid landing the Cheltenham Gold Cup, and the battle between Marling and Selkirk for the Sussex Stakes.

Those were real pinnacles of excitement and memory. This was very much of that level.

The others were, predominantly, achievements by horses in individual races, and to watch a jockey doing what Dettori did yesterday was that bit different. Seven varied horses, seven races, all sorts of tactics in all sorts of circumstances – the more you think about it, the more you have to admire it.

A fourth winner with Decorated Hero was exciting, fifth with Fatefully really something, sixth on Lochangel meant that Frankie would have gone through the card in the old days of only six races, and the excitement and anticipation just never stopped building.

The crowd loved it, just like Dettori loved them. His exuberant enthusiasm was so much part of the celebrations and the audience responded to his reaction with unrestrained excitement.

You just don't see scenes like this very often, if ever. Racing remains a pretty staid old game, and is not necessarily any the worse for that, but this was a time to let the hair down.

People were already starting to do that with a circuit to go in the closing two-mile handicap. As Dettori passed the post in front on Fujiyama Crest on the first circuit they gave him a huge cheer, but I doubt if many anticipated that he would be there again a mile and six furlongs later.

But he was, and didn't everyone love it. They rushed off the stands towards the unsaddling enclosure as if they knew they had seen something they would never witness again. For sure, they knew that nobody had ever been part of something like this before.

To have seen such a hugely popular man and superb ambassador for racing pull off such a wonderful feat was a privilege. I was there, and I wouldn't have missed it for the world.

The achievement was so enormous and the climax came so late in the afternoon for the Sunday papers that the impact and the reportage spilled over into Monday. It gave us all – even Frankie – a chance to catch our breath.

'It only really hit me in the morning afterwards what an amazing achievement it was. I don't have to tell you: I'm overwhelmed by it.

I drove straight to the newsagent and bought every paper. Then my fiancée Catherine and myself sat down and went through them all. Then it hit me. It looked more difficult than it did the night before.

Looking back, when I went to the races I was just concentrating on the Queen Elizabeth. I had a couple of other chances but as the afternoon went on it became a dream and, at the end, a fairytale.

Nobody could believe it and I was the first not to believe it. After my sixth winner I was presented with champagne for equalling the record and I thought, 'Great!'

But we came to the last and I saw my horse was a 12-1 chance in the papers. I later found out he was 2-1 favourite, and when I saw Teletext when I got home I saw I'd cost the bookies £18 million. I thought there might be a hitman waiting for me at the track today!

I'm sorry I cost them so much but it was good that people won money betting on me. I don't think it will ever happen again, but I'm pleased those faithfuls who like to back my horses got a big reward. Tomorrow I'll be on television to meet the person who won half a million.

But to win seven out of seven at Ascot is almost impossible. I beat 98 horses and I'm still in shock.

From the fourth to the seventh I can't really remember anything. I was just floating. I was just dragged left, right and centre. It was just staggering. I don't know where I was or what I was riding, but I kept on winning.

But the most enjoyable time I had was when I was cantering past the stands for the last race and 20,000 people stood up and clapped me and Fujiyama Crest. It was very emotional.

The last furlong was like a mile and I can tell you Pat [Eddery, on runner-up Northern Fleet] gave the second a good go to beat me.

When we crossed the line I made a big scream and lost a little bit of my voice. It was a dream come true and to see all the people afterwards was fantastic.

I was exhausted mentally and physically last night. I didn't leave the track until 7pm and I got home [to Newmarket] about 9pm. I picked up Catherine and we went around to [Godolphin racing manager] Simon Crisford's and had a drink. We watched the replay of the races and hung about for an hour but I was dead tired and we just went home.

I knew I had to ride again the next day and it's very hard to go out and not let yourself down. I wanted a clear mind, but I watched Arsenal's two goals!

I think I had more messages on the answerphone than Bill Clinton when he became President. I had a lot but I left them until the morning because I didn't have time to hear them all.

I also spoke to my dad, who is in Gran Canaria, where he can only get three English newspapers and Teletext. Obviously he was concerned about Mark Of Esteem, so he checked the text and saw I'd won the first three races.

He was delighted, but when he checked again later and my stepmother asked how I'd got on, he said, 'There must be something wrong with the Teletext, it isn't working. There must be something wrong – he's got all seven winners!'

That was a classic. I just imagine the picture.

[Trainer] Les Benton also called me from Australia to tell me it was on the front page over there and I also had messages from the States, so I think the whole racing world knows.

I was delighted to see I made 9.15pm on the *Nine O'Clock News* – that's probably the closest I can get to nine o'clock.

It has been a great day today[Sunday] as well. At 7am a man from the *Daily Mail* barged into my house. I said, 'OK – do you want to come into my bedroom?'

I'm sad the dream stopped in the first race, as I wanted to win the race for the crowd and keep the dream going. Unfortunately it was over, but everybody was kind of waiting for me to ride a winner so I'm glad I could pull it off in the end.

I believe in God, and sometimes he's on your side. Yesterday he was definitely on my side. It's a privilege to be associated with such a great sport like racing, with so many great people.

I'm just doing my job winning races. I'll be glad to eat something tonight – I haven't really eaten for a couple of days – then I'll go and put my feet up and relax.

But after yesterday I'm on a high for a week. I don't even mind going to Bath tomorrow!'

It had been a racing feat like no other, and meant that racing made the headlines for the very best of reasons:

Just in case anyone needed reminding of Frankie Dettori's unbelievable achievement, it was there yesterday in all of Britain's Sunday newspapers.

It usually takes a major race like the Grand National – even the Derby struggled for significant coverage this year – to ensure such attention. The splash of headlines and colour devoted to Dettori made it clear what an impact he had made on the world of sport, not just racing.

The *Sunday Express* called it a 'Racing Sensation', and it was.

Also sensational was the publicity skills demonstrated by bookmakers, who proved quicker out of the stalls than any of Dettori's mounts at Ascot on Saturday.

Three! Frankie celebrates as Mark Of Esteem beats Bosra Sham

Incredibly, the *Sunday Express*'s main news report on the front page of its sports supplement quoted Warwick Bartlett, the chairman of the British Betting Offices' Association, in the third paragraph – a long way higher than any Dettori remark.

Bartlett claimed that thirty to forty shops would close as a result of Dettori's 25,095-1 seven-timer. To come up with such a figure within hours of Fujiyama Crest's victory is a tribute to Bartlett's economic skills. It was a perfect journalistic equivalent of the dreaded 'soundbite'.

Elsewhere in the *Express*, Jonathan Powell wrote: 'Nothing in racing could possibly match the towering performance of Frankie Dettori at Ascot yesterday.'

That was a sentiment repeated elsewhere.

In the *Sunday Telegraph*, Brough Scott wrote: 'Never seen the like of it. Never heard anything on a racetrack to equal it. It was the most exhilarating, most 'to think that I was ever there' applause the game will ever see.'

Much was made, also, of Dettori's unique personality. He 'surpassed the greatest names in the history of the sport,' said John Karter in the Sunday Times. Dettori is a man whose 'showmanship has enabled him to transcend racing like no rider before him.'

The News Of The World devoted the bulk of its back page to what Dettori did at Ascot, and inside reporter Colin Cooper wrote: 'Bookies were facing ruin last night as jubilant punters queued up to collect huge sums on Frankie Dettori's magnificent seven at Ascot.'

Graham Rock in *The Observer* described Saturday's events as 'giving British bookmakers their worst day since betting shops were legalised in the early Sixties . . . A few bookmakers will have been destroyed.'

Racing is not like other sports since its followers are involved with much more than just enthusiasm – most of them are betting their hard-earned cash. By Monday there were monster tales of joy and disaster and, just for once, the bookies 'Wolf, Wolf' stories of record losses were all too painfully close to the truth, as Nick Godfrey described.

Four! Decorated Hero turns the competitive Tote Festival Handicap into a procession.

Bookmakers said yesterday that Frankie Dettori's unprecedented seven-timer at Ascot on Saturday may have lost them as much as £20 million in the short term.

Estimates of the pay-out are inevitably imprecise, with bookmakers keen to play up the 'damage' they have suffered before the money starts to flow back into their tills.

Off-course firms, one of whom described the Italian's Saturday spree as having caused 'the worst day in bookmaking history', started to claw back the deficit yesterday, when Sunday trading appeared brisker than usual on the back of the Dettori bandwagon.

But yesterday's trade was small beer compared to Saturday's losses, which hit bookmakers both on- and off-course and left one spokesman claiming – somewhat improbably – that thirty to forty shops would be forced to close as a result.

As the dust settled yesterday, estimates of the cost to Britain's bookmakers of multiple bets on Dettori's winners ranged between £15 million and £20 million.

'I would make a "guesstimate" of £20 million,' said Coral spokesman Rob Hartnett, while Ladbrokes felt £15 million was closer to the mark.

To put the figure into context, bookmakers expect to take around £60 million on Grand National day, by far the no.1 day's turnover of the year. Not all that is profit, of course.

All layers were licking their wounds yesterday. William Hill, the country's second biggest firm after Ladbrokes, admitted to losses of £8 million on its own, while one senior on-course layer, who wished to remain unnamed, claimed that as many as forty per cent of his colleagues had failed to stand at Sunday's meeting, following Saturday's business.

Rails bookmaker Gary Wiltshire, whose losses ran well into six figures, reckoned he and his colleagues had lost £2 million – most of it to hedging bets from other bookmakers – on Fujiyama Crest's historic victory alone.

Ladbrokes spokesman Mike Dillon said: 'The estimates were £10 million yesterday, and they are more like £15 million today.

It's difficult to put a figure on it because, by definition, many of the punters who have won are small punters and we will not know the real effects for a couple of days.'

However, Dillon argued that Dettori's exploits, however costly in the short term, might eventually reap a reward in betting shops. 'It's great for the business as a whole,' he said.

The effect of the big off-course firms passing their liabilities on to the layers at the track shortened the price of Dettori's mounts on Saturday.

'We put £100,000 on the last race and it was insufficient,' said William Hill spokesman Mike Burton.

Colleague David Hood described Saturday as the blackest in bookmaking history. 'It's our equivalent of the stock-market crash,' he said.

On course at Ascot, the beleaguered Wiltshire spoke for the majority of the rails bookmakers. 'It was disastrous for everybody,' he said.

Senior Tattersalls layer Barry Dennis said: 'We were open-mouthed, gobsmacked. It can never happen again in our lifetime. It was my biggest ever losing day.

That Monday had so much talk of records that it was easy to miss a report that trainer Martin Pipe had split with jockey David Bridgwater, and a young man called McCoy was favourite to take over. No jumping record would be safe.

At the Racing Post *we have a duty to put all records into perspective – which is why historian John Randall's verdict on 'The Magnificent Seven' was required reading at the start of the week.*

Racing results have been reliably chronicled since 1727, so it is always dangerous to say that a particular achievement has never been bettered or equalled.

Virtually everything has been done before, yet Frankie Dettori's clean sweep of the seven races at the Ascot Festival on Saturday was an epoch-making feat, on a par with Michael Dickinson training the first five in the 1983 Cheltenham Gold Cup.

Never before had a jockey ridden seven winners on one card in Britain, and we may never witness it again in our lifetimes. Indeed, only two jockeys, Gordon Richards and Alec Russell, have ever gone through the card on a six-race programme.

Ironically, Pat Eddery, who chased Dettori home in three races at Ascot, was, until Saturday, the only jockey to win seven races in a day in Britain. They comprised three in the afternoon at Newmarket and four in the evening at Newcastle on 26 June 1992, when the Irishman had a total of eleven rides.

But until Dettori's grand slam, the jockey who went closest to winning seven races on one card was George Fordham.

At Stockbridge on 18 June 1867, Fordham won on six of his seven mounts and deadheated on the other (an odds-on favourite), only to lose the run-off ...

Frankie was now famous as no jockey had ever been before. But we all know that fame can be a fickle friend, and there was perceptive prophecy as well as admiration in Paul Haigh's Monday reflections which closed our thoughts on what had happened on that Ascot Saturday afternoon.

Seven up! Fujiyama Crest takes Frankie into the history books.

Something funny happened yesterday. At 2 o'clock they ran a race at Ascot and Frankie Dettori didn't win it.

It would be wrong to describe the crowd's reaction as one of shock. But it would certainly be fair to say that this strange event provided a demonstration to some that the game isn't quite as simple as it might have appeared on D-Day.

Somewhere, no doubt, there are a few first-time racegoers who attended our premier course on Saturday and went away to tell their friends how British racing works: 'Well, they all go down to the post and they all start at the same time. Then Frankie's horse goes to the front. After it passes the post he punches the air, gulps the air and jumps in the air, and we all go off to collect.'

We've been waiting for a genuine 24-carat hero for a while now. But it didn't occur to many of us that the hero might be one who could talk. If it had been a horse we'd have known how to sell it.

Always assuming the owners were prepared to let it run a few times, we'd have known how to help it promote the game for all it was worth.

Cigar, if nothing else, would have provided us with a model to work from when it came to making the flagship work for the

greater glory of the sport. What racing has to do now is work out how it can maximise the impact of this great jockey on the general public.

We probably don't have to worry about spoiling him. This is a man who embraces success like an old chum and controls any tendency to self-adoration with frequent references to what he has plenty of reason to regard as a benevolent deity.

The great thing about Frankie is that he embraces everyone like an old chum. The thing that makes him such an attractive personality and should make him – there's no escaping the already-clichéd phrase – 'such a wonderful ambassador for racing' is that he isn't in the slightest bit self-conscious about the joy that victory brings him and isn't in the slightest bit grudging about sharing that joy.

But while he isn't going to be spoilt now, he might well find himself hemmed in by what he has become. If you want to look for a comparable situation you might like to consider Brian Lara, the cricketer who altered all perceptions about what was possible in his sport.

Lara was – and probably is – a lovely chap too: a kind, gentle, level-headed man who had time for everyone and who wore a dazzling smile as his customary expression.

But the time-managers got to him – the men who see a hero not as an individual but a business opportunity. They organised him, told him what he was worth. And in the space of a couple of years the outward signs changed. Suddenly under the pressure of demands for interviews, the pressure to sell his contracts and endorsements, to sell himself as dearly as his advisers wished, seemed to get to him and he seemed to become introverted and self-obsessed.

People will come to Frankie now and tell him how rich they can make him. (He might point out to them that he's happy already and likely to become as rich as any normal person should want to be simply from the continuing exercise of his talent.) They will point out to him that there are only 24 hours even in his day and that his time is money.

They will not point out that if he succumbs to their arguments he will become a commodity, and that we can all kiss goodbye to the sunny spontaneity that's made us all warm to him.

ABOVE: When Ascot memorabilia was auctioned for charity before rebuilding the royal course began, larger-than-life bookie Gary Wilsthire picked up an appropriate souvenir of his disastrous day.

RIGHT: A moment of calm before the bedlam in the winner's enclosure.

The man himself is tremendously keen that his success should be of benefit not just to himself but to the sport as a whole. This was one of the themes he kept repeating in the aftermath of his triumph: 'Let's show everyone that this is the greatest sport there is.'

I wouldn't pretend to have any cast-iron answers, but the question that should be taxing everyone who cares about racing now is: how can we make the most of this precious windfall asset and help him to do for the sport exactly what he wants.

Fujiyama Crest in honourable retirement with the man he made famous.

ON THE EDGE

*O*vernight Frankie had become the most popular man in
Britain, and not just to punter Darren Yates, to whom he
presented the £550,000 William Hill cheque on the GMTV
sofa. There was a telegram from the Queen, an interview on Parkinson,
a reception at 10 Downing Street and a host spot on Top of the Pops.
There were cars from Alfa Romeo, sponsorships from McDonalds to The
Tote to T-Mobile, and on the track in November there was the biggest
money win of his career to date, Singspiel winning the £1,093,662
Japan Cup in Tokyo.

Next summer Singspiel won the Coronation Cup at Epsom and after
struggling in the soft at Ascot he came good so handsomely at York that
Frankie was making claims that rather belied the colt's comparatively
slender frame.

Tim Richards reported:

Singspiel bowed out of European racing with Frankie Dettori
describing him as 'the undisputed heavyweight champion of
the world' after a gala performance in yesterday's Juddmonte
International at York.

With odds-on favourite Bosra Sham disappointing in last place
after ripping off a shoe, the globe-trotting colt took star billing under
a super-confident Dettori and is now heading for a grand finale in the
Breeders' Cup Turf or Classic at Hollywood Park, where the curtain
will come down on a phenomenal career.

Dettori described the colt, who has also won the Canadian
International, Japan Cup, Dubai World Cup and Coronation Cup
as the best he has ever ridden. His more conservative but very
professional trainer Michael Stoute admitted: 'He's certainly one of
the best I've had.'

Singspiel cruised through to gobble up the pacemaking Benny The
Dip at the three-furlong marker. And he did it in a matter of strides to
turn one of Europe's top races into an exhibition.

Desert King, the Irish Derby winner, was one and a half lengths
back in second place with Benny The Dip, the Derby hero,
another one and a half lengths adrift in third. Bosra Sham, minus

*Rubbing shoulders with another
legend: Frankie with rock superstar
Ronnie Wood.*

the shoe, was a length and a quarter further back last of the four runners.

For the winners, however, it was time to celebrate and Dettori did not disappoint his thousands of followers.

He augmented a tumultuous reception by continually waving to the crowds. He threw his whip over their heads, aiming into the hands of valet Dave Currie leaning out of the jockeys' room window. It was the only target he missed.

The famous Dettori leap from Singspiel's back into owner Sheikh Mohammed's waiting arms was followed by the rider kissing the lens of the television camera attempting to capture his performance, which by now had nearly reached Oscar-winning proportions.

'He's the undisputed heavyweight champion of the world,' enthused Dettori. 'He has beaten France's Helissio, the Americans' Sandpit and Siphon, and now Bosra Sham and these two Derby winners. This is a great year for older horses and he's the best of them.'

He added: 'When we got to the straight I thought we'd make a race of it. Three and a half furlongs out I said "Go!" and he did. You saw what happened.'

Sadly Singspiel fractured a cannon bone preparing for the Breeders' Cup and never ran again.

Singspiel wins the 1997 Juddmonte International from Desert King and Benny The Dip.

*Cape Verdi cruises home in the 1998
One Thousand Guineas.*

*Frankie did, and the 1998 British season opened with a runaway win
in the One Thousand Guineas for Cape Verdi. But it was Royal Ascot
which gave Dettori the summer headlines. First in the Gold Cup with
Kayf Tara. Alastair Down was there.*

When the Dettori first-born sees the light of day among its many
Christian names – Gianfranco, Lanfranco II, Godolphin, Loadsalire,
Gosden – the word 'Ascot' is also bound to figure.

It was here that he netted that magic seven, a feat for which punters
will always love him because for just a few happy hours he put the
bookmakers on the endangered species list somewhere between the
okapi and the black rhino. And yesterday this course once again proved
a joyful stage for him with a treble that will have meant a great deal to
him on more levels than one and brought his tally for the meeting to six.

He opened hostilities with an easy victory on Bahr in the
Ribblesdale, a race she should have won on the book, although

you are always taking a chance bouncing an Oaks filly into the Ribblesdale.

There is nothing of Bahr to look at but that slight frame is very gritty. She whizzed in here and Godolphin now has three weeks to get her back to her peak for the Irish Oaks.

'No mistake this time,' said Frankie as he brought her in, referring to his opinion that Mick Kinane might have outwitted him in the Oaks, although he may not be giving himself the benefit of the doubt.

But the race where Dettori really excelled yesterday was the Gold Cup, in which he denied Double Trigger a victory that would have had the crowd cheering themselves hoarse with a perfectly judged ride on Kayf Tara.

There was every chance Kayf Tara wouldn't get the trip and Dettori settled him immediately and wasted not an ounce of effort or yard of ground in smuggling him into the race before stalking Double Trigger from the turn and running him out of it close home.

The beauty of it lay in the timing. With Double Trigger on a going day, Frankie delayed hitting the front until just inside the final furlong, and the way Trigger stuck at him and fought back you can't help feeling that if Frankie had taken it up just a few strides earlier then the Johnston horse might have battled him out of it.

By the end of the meeting things had got even better. Richard Griffiths told the story.

Frankie Dettori waited until the last race yesterday to seal a truly memorable Royal Ascot with a seventh winner, which gave him the highest total since Pat Eddery in 1989.

After the setback of Swain's defeat in the Hardwicke, Dettori returned in style to swoop on 12-1 shot Dovedon Star in the Queen Alexandra Stakes – a victory that scuppered the last of the remaining 70p of bets remaining on the jackpot.

Dettori was soon orchestrating proceedings in the winner's enclosure once more, as he performed his second flying dismount of the week.

'It is great – fantastic,' Dettori said. A treble yesterday would have given him an unprecedented nine winners, but he added: 'Seven winners is a lot and it has been a great week. Swain ran a bit flat but apart from that, it was magnificent.

'Godolphin has had a marvellous meeting and for me there is no place like Ascot. They should close down all the other 58 courses and just have races here,' joked Dettori, who will receive his second successive London Clubs Trophy from the Queen Mother at Ascot today.

'I really do love the place. It has been very good to me.'

It was at Ascot in September 1996 that Dettori became a sporting legend with his seven-timer, but his enthusiasm for the Royal Meeting remains particularly strong. 'It's such a great meeting. It's exciting for everyone and I just want to carry on riding winners here,' he said.

Although he was on Daylami when stablemate Faithful Son won the Prince of Wales's Stakes, Dettori and Godolphin got off to a great start when Intikhab won the Queen Anne Stakes.

On Thursday Bahr gained ample reward for her Oaks defeat – when Dettori felt he was at fault – in the Ribblesdale.

Highlight of the week was Dettori's Gold Cup success on Kayf Tara. The jockey has won the race three times, having previously been successful with Drum Taps and Classic Cliché.

'I think I had forgotten what it was like to win the Gold Cup but it was just as nice,' Dettori said. 'After two and a half miles it is just sheer delight when you hit that winning post.'

There was also a bit of fortune about the third leg of his Thursday treble, Rhapsodist in the Chesham Stakes.

'I was going to ride Compton Admiral [the runner-up] because John [Gosden] was worried about the soft ground for Rhapsodist, but I was able to change my plans,' Dettori said.

Gosden also provided Dettori with Plan-B in Tuesday's Britannia Handicap, while the other member of his septet was Bint Allayl in the Queen Mary.

Swain was set to be Frankie's horse for the autumn. Together they had taken the King George at Ascot and the Irish Champion at

Swain powers clear of High-Rise (right) and Royal Anthem in the 1998 King George VI and Queen Elizabeth Stakes.

Leopardstown, and all looked set fair for the Breeders' Cup in Kentucky. American racing's end-of-season jamboree had already given Frankie good days and bad ones, but 1998 was the worst.

Jon Lees and David Ashforth shared the byline.

Frankie Dettori has come under intense fire after an extraordinary riding performance aboard Swain in Saturday's Breeders' Cup Classic which saw the dual King George winner beaten a length into third.

Even Godolphin trainer Saeed bin Suroor yesterday attributed the narrow defeat in the world's richest race to 'a mistake' from the Italian.

American journalists were rather more trenchant in their criticism, however, claiming Swain would have won had any other rider involved been on his back, after the horse had veered across the track under a fierce left-handed whip drive from Europe's most celebrated jockey.

Swain's performance had promised to redeem what had hitherto proved a dismal day at Churchill Downs from a European standpoint, with no other raiders placed in the seven-race extravaganza.

However, all that were left were 'what-might-have-beens' after the six-year-old was beaten three-quarters of a length and a neck behind Awesome Again – trained by Essex-born Patrick Byrne – and Dubai World Cup winner Silver Charm in a race billed as the strongest renewal ever run.

Dettori immediately blamed lights on the trackside for Swain's dramatic change of course, claiming he would have won if Swain had not been distracted.

But after reviewing the race several times Saeed bin Suroor, in a frank analysis, made it clear he did not accept the excuse.

'I can't see that the grandstand lights were to blame,' said the trainer. 'All the people watching the race there and on TV all over the world know he made a mistake. But that happens in a race.

'It's a shame. Frankie is a big name and he's our jockey. At the same time, I would like to see him ride better than this.

'I know he is a brilliant jockey. He is one of the best jockeys in Europe. It is normal to make a mistake.'

Domestic turf writers had little time for the Italian's explanation either. 'Dettori's excuse was a lot more creative than his ride,' wrote Vic Ziegel of the New York Daily News. 'Maybe he will have a better story by the time he gets home.'

Bill Finley, writing in the same paper, said 'Swain probably would have won if anybody but Frankie Dettori was on his back.'

The local Lexington Herald-Leader reported: 'Swain went practically to the grandstand under a volley of left-handed whipping. Dettori was flailing away with a left-sided whip while Swain drifted further and further to the right.'

Dettori had twice been dropped on his way to the start by Swain, who took exception to his rider tapping him on his neck.

But once the race started the pair were always well placed. Swain angled to the outside on the home turn to prepare for a final stretch challenge.

As he looked poised for another duel with Dubai World Cup conqueror Silver Charm, Dettori switched his whip to his left hand and, with his head down, delivered a barrage of blows. He was seen to strike Swain twelve times, sometimes out of rhythm with the horse.

Swain edged further and further across the track, and only when Dettori put his whip down did the horse start to run straight again. But the damage had been done and the race lost.

On his return, Dettori threw his hands up and complained to Sheikh Mohammed: 'I had the race won and then he saw the lights and then boom! We lost two lengths going across the track.

'The ride was good until he saw the lights in the last 100 yards and he veered right and it cost me the race.

The post-mortem on Churchill Downs.

'He's not used to that kind of thing. When he hit the front, he saw those lights on the left. I was only beaten just over three-quarters of a length and it cost me two lengths.'

At that point Sheikh Mohammed seemed to accept Dettori's assertion and claimed Swain, who now retires to stud in Kentucky, was the moral victor. 'He was the best horse on the day,' said the Sheikh. He was one of the best winners we've had and certainly the best horse here.'

It has been a bad week of globe-hopping for Dettori, who also received his share of flak from Australian professionals over a ride considered ill-judged on Annus Mirabilis in the Grade 1 Mackinnon Stakes.

Bin Suroor reaffirmed his faith in Dettori as Godolphin's jockey. He said: 'Frankie is our jockey. We like him, we love him. We need him to stay at the top all of the time.

'At the same time I understand Frankie can't do everything right all the time. This is racing.

'This was our best chance. It is very hard to find a horse like Swain and he was coming from behind to win. I am really sorry for Frankie.

'Swain has won two King Georges, a Coronation Cup, Irish Champion Stakes, second in the World Cup. He can handle any ground and surface. He was a brilliant horse.

'I am not upset. I understand in racing you can't win all the time. But I wish we'd done something better.'

Frankie got so depressed afterwards that he even thought of quitting Godolphin. Good job he didn't, as 1999 was the year their operation really took off as a global force. They won eighteen Group 1s and Frankie was on thirteen of them.

The three-year-old Dubai Millennium was the emerging superstar, and when he rocketed home in the Queen Elizabeth II Stakes at Ascot, Sheikh Mohammed said he was 'the best we have ever had.' But it was the old grey Daylami who was the mainstay, winning the Coronation Cup, King George and Irish Champion, and even when he blew out in

the Arc, Frankie only waited three days for the richest of compensation – for his wife Catherine produced Leo, their first-born.

Even then Daylami had one more favour to pay, to lay the Breeders' Cup ghost that had haunted Frankie since the Swain debacle of a year ago.

Jon Lees reported.

Daylami rampages clear to win the 1999 Breeders' Cup Turf … and (overleaf) Frankie reaches for the sky.

Europe's ten-year wait for a Breeders' Cup victory in Florida ended in dramatic fashion on Saturday when Daylami and Frankie Dettori combined to engineer a brilliant success for Godolphin at Gulfstream Park.

A sequence of 44 consecutive losers at 'Graveyard Park' had mounted race by race until the remarkable grey surged up the finishing straight to capture the $2million Breeders' Cup Turf, a victory of huge personal significance for Dettori.

Daylami will now be retired and is due at Gilltown Stud in Ireland tomorrow.

The five-year-old's eleventh career win enabled a jubilant Dettori to exorcise a personal ghost after his much criticised performance on Swain at last year's Breeders' Cup, a bitter experience that was still clearly uppermost in his mind twelve months on.

Dettori justifiably milked his 'second-best moment after the Magnificent Seven at Ascot'.

In addition to the trademark flying dismount, the Italian also hurled his helmet skywards, jumping wildly about, and shouting: 'Come on, me!' He threw the garland of orchids reserved for the winning horse around his own neck in delight.

Not finished yet, he then teased the 45,124 crowd by calling out: 'What about me?'

Channel 4 pundit John McCririck, working for America's NBC television, told him: 'You showed America.'

And didn't Frankie love telling us?

'Revenge is a plate best served cold and today mine is freezing. I'm glad to put the ghost of Swain behind me after last year.

It took me six months to get over the Swain affair. Everyone was judging me on one ride. They tried to bury me.

I made a mistake which was fair enough, but you don't write off a ten-year career on that.

I was in tears in the last 100 yards, thinking, I can't believe I'm going to win.'

I felt every sort of emotion – joy, tears, happiness, sadness. Even now I have to pinch myself. I don't believe it's true.

Everyone tried to kill me last year, but it made me a stronger person. There are a lot more important things to life. You have to turn a page and move on.

All the press eyes were on me, just waiting for me to mess up. Daylami came to the rescue. I redeemed myself today. I was feeling the pressure. I was fine, but when I got to the races my heart started pumping. I knew I had three great rides and I was hoping to God nothing would stand in my path to cause trouble.

The first two rides, Lend A Hand and Zomaradah, knocked on the door and it didn't open, but finally it did for Daylami.

This is the second best moment of my career after the 'Magnificent Seven' at Ascot.

Daylami is a fantastic horse. He was a machine today, and he's the best horse I've ever ridden. He's got a big heart, and really tries for you. He's a joy to ride. They don't come very often and I'm going to miss him. I gave him a good pat after the race. He's done me proud.'

No horse has ever lived up to his name better than the way Dubai Millennium won the Dubai World Cup in the year 2000. It was not just that he broke the two-minute barrier for the 2000 metres under the desert moon, it was the way he did it.

Frankie himself summed up a magical evening.

'No words can describe this performance tonight but I will try – it was unbelievable. He's definitely the best horse I've ridden. With him, it's just sheer ability, power, speed and stamina – it's unbelievable.

I was worried about making the running at one stage, but he has a mind of his own and today he wanted to go – I wasn't going to stop him! As I get a bit more experience of dirt racing I'm learning that it's different to turf racing in that you can't afford to fight them. He wanted to go, so I said OK, let's go.

I managed to get a little bit of daylight just before the straight, then when I got to the furlong marker, the crowd started clapping. Obviously they thought I'd won, so I stood up to have a look at them – I nearly broke my neck! At that point I almost had tears of disbelief.

We always knew we had a good horse, though for the last few weeks it's been scary for us because he's been showing us so much at home and we just hoped he would be able to reproduce it on the track. But I didn't expect a performance like that.

This has been a big night for me. I've been working for Godolphin and Sheikh Mohammed for five years and this is our big day; my name wasn't there yet – but now we've got it up there.

I was speaking before the race, looking at all my rides, and I said we have four or five horses running in each of them so I've probably picked the wrong one, but I'm definitely on the right one in the last, no doubt about that!

Now he's four, Dubai Millennium is stronger and more mature. But he never stops surprising me. On grass he's got an amazing turn of foot, but on dirt his speed is unbelievable – he doesn't come off the bridle. I would prefer to ride him on turf, but if he keeps reproducing this sort of performance I won't mind riding him on dirt!

I'm a very lucky young man. I have a fantastic job working for Sheikh Mohammed and a wonderful team at Godolphin who work very hard. I'm the guy who tends to get all the credit, but it's a great team effort and, let's be honest, tonight anyone could have won on him.'

In hindsight there is some irony in a couple of the news stories we carried that spring. In April, Frankie was talking of the strain of travelling and the likelihood of the need to stop at forty. In May he was appearing on Songs of Praise *and saying that he would always need help from the Almighty. On the first day of June he was going to need all the help he could get, as Tony Elves and Richard Griffiths reported.*

Frankie Dettori told hospital visitors last night it was 'a miracle' he was still alive following the plane crash in Newmarket yesterday that also involved Ray Cochrane and caused the death of the pilot.

The two jockeys took off from Newmarket for Goodwood, but their plane was forced to crash-land soon after.

The pilot struggled for control of the Piper Seneca, but managed to land while narrowly missing the Devil's Dyke which separates Newmarket's two racecourses.

The plane nose-dived into the ground, causing the pilot's death, while Dettori and Cochrane escaped through the small luggage compartment at the back of the plane.

Dettori's business manager, Peter Burrell, who visited the jockey at Cambridge's Addenbrooke's Hospital, said: 'Another four or five seconds and they would have been killed.'

Cochrane, who asked for no details of his condition to be released, had screamed at Dettori to leave the plane before he returned to try and drag out the pilot. Cochrane was unable to do so because the plane was engulfed in flames.

Dettori, who said his immediate concern was for the pilot and his family, suffered a broken right ankle in the crash plus 'numerous cuts and bruises' to his face and body. He may also need surgery on one of his thumbs.

Both men were detained overnight at Addenbrooke's, where they had been taken by helicopter after the accident.

Dettori's wife, Catherine, raced to the hospital to be with him, while their young son Leonardo was looked after at home.

The Italian was later visited by his close friend Colin Rate, who was apprenticed to Luca Cumani at the same time as Dettori.

Cochrane was visited by his wife, Anne.

At around 4.45pm yesterday Burrell left Dettori's side to explain his condition to the reporters waiting outside the hospital.

He said: 'Frankie is very smashed up and has numerous cuts and lacerations to his face and body and to his hands.'

Dettori had to have several stitches to his face last night.

Burrell added: 'Frankie is at pains to say how sorry he is about the pilot. His spirits are fine, he's a very strong man – he's just very sorry about the pilot.'

The wreckage.

Burrell said that Dettori knew the pilot well and flew with him on a near-daily basis. 'From what I can gather, the pilot did a great job to achieve what he achieved. He was fighting for control of the plane. It took off as normal, but was forced to land. Fortunately it missed the dyke between the two courses, otherwise it could have been a lot worse.'

Dettori was conscious throughout the ordeal and Burrell said: 'He's very lucky to be lying in bed. I was shocked when I saw Frankie and realised how lucky he and Ray are to get out of this. Frankie said he doesn't care if he's in hospital for seven days, he knows how lucky he is. He thinks it's a miracle.'

Burrell added that Dettori, who was due to ride Best Of The Bests for Godolphin in the Vodafone Derby a week tomorrow, is likely to be out of action until August.

'He's definitely out of the Derby. I shouldn't think he'll be back racing until mid-August. A broken ankle will take time to heal.

'The Derby will have to wait until next year. I imagine that once he has got out of here and settled down, he will go on holiday.'

The crash scene, which was attended by five fire engines, an all-terrain vehicle, ten police vehicles, three ambulances and an air ambulance, was cordoned off and the press were kept about 250 yards away from the wreckage.

The mangled aircraft was partially shielded from view by a fire engine and there was a marked reluctance for either police or fire officers to say anything.

A groom from the National Stud had witnessed the accident and is reported as seeing petrol leaking from the plane, which had taken off before veering sharply to its right, across Devil's Dyke, and crashing to the ground.

The scene was one of total devastation with the plane, apart from the tailpiece and propeller, which was lodged in the ground, the only recognisable parts.

Peter Ludford, Duty Division Officer for Suffolk Fire Service, said: 'The emergency services were alerted by someone with a mobile telephone and one of our engines from Newmarket was very soon in attendance.

'Looking at the site, there was a fairly severe spillage of aviation fuel in the area around the plane and it's lucky that anyone has got out alive.'

Miles Littlewort, chief executive of the National Stud, which adjoins the July course, attended the accident and said: 'They're both incredibly lucky because there wasn't much of the plane left.

'It's an absolute miracle that either person got out alive.'

A day later Catherine Dettori told Tony Elves, our man in Newmarket, how for Frankie, Ray Cochrane had been nothing less than a miracle worker.

'Ray Cochrane helped pull Frankie Dettori clear of the burning wreck of their light aircraft before going back to try to save the pilot', Dettori's wife Catherine said yesterday.

Mrs Dettori, 26, holding the couple's baby boy, Leonardo, in her arms, gave details of the crash to reporters outside Addenbrooke's Hospital in Cambridge, where the two jockeys remained yesterday in the wake of Thursday's accident.

'It's all very shocking,' she said. 'We can't really get our heads around it. Frankie phoned me. He just said, "We've had a crash and the pilot's dead. We're at the July Course."

'I just couldn't believe it. It was surreal, really. I was in the house doing other things. I shot straight down there to see him.'

On the immediate aftermath of the crash, which killed pilot Patrick Mackey, Mrs Dettori said: 'From what I can gather, the plane was bouncing on the ground after they took off. I think Frankie thinks one of the propellers was caught on the edge as it was bouncing.

'The pilot was amazing. He got them over a bank. Ray was amazing. That's why he got a burned face.

'Obviously, he got Frankie away from the aeroplane. Frankie couldn't move on his leg. Ray went back to try to get the pilot.'

Flames were said to have beaten back Cochrane, who suffered burns and a suspected broken nose, while Dettori fractured an ankle and also suffered burns.

Frankie on the day he left hospital.

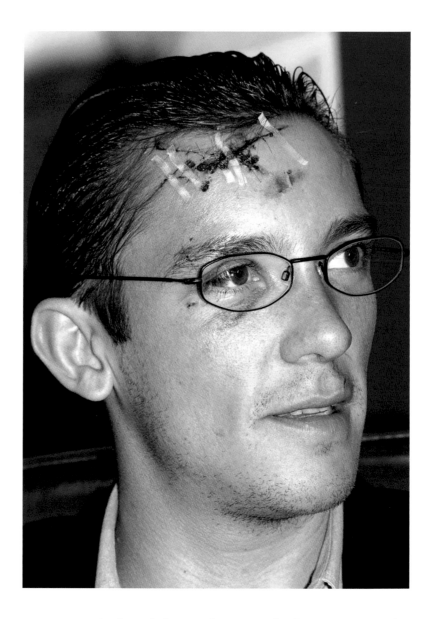

Mrs Dettori, whose father Professor Twink Allen is a respected equine scientist, added: 'All our thoughts are with the pilot's family.

'It may be bad for me, but it's much worse for the pilot's wife.

'I can just go home. I've still got a husband.'

She added: 'The pilot was a lovely guy.'

Asked if the recent air crash involving Formula 1 racing driver David Coulthard had made her think twice about her husband flying, Mrs Dettori said: 'You just never think it's going to happen to you or anyone you know.

'You know there's always a risk with these planes, but they have to fly. You just have to get to work every day.

'I definitely think there are too many meetings for them. It just adds to the risks.'

A week on, Frankie was coming out. And this would be a very different Frankie from any we had seen before. Jon Lees filed the story.

'Right now, the Derby means nothing,' an emotional Frankie Dettori said yesterday in a harrowing account of last week's Newmarket plane crash, which he described as 'beyond scary', writes Jon Lees.

Cut, bruised and visibly shaken while speaking to reporters on his discharge from hospital, he vowed to take as much time as he needed to recover from the mental and physical scars of Thursday's accident, in which the pilot Patrick Mackey was killed and Dettori and fellow passenger Ray Cochrane were both injured.

Dettori, sombre, reflective and thankful just to be alive, said that racing mattered little to him right now, and indicated that his darkest moments may still be ahead, giving rise to fresh speculation as to how long it will be before he returns to the saddle.

'If I never win a race again it doesn't matter,' he said, adding: 'I've got my life and I've got that to look forward to. I'll probably come back and give it a go when I'm mentally ready.

'I'm 29 years old, I have my wife and young son and I would like to spend a bit of time with them and get myself together and think about it. Then I will come back to racing when I feel ready.'

A bespectacled Dettori, speaking on what he described as 'the fifth day of my new life', has yet to win the Derby and would have had strong claims on Godolphin's Best Of The Bests on Saturday.

He recognised it is 'obviously the biggest race, and the only one I haven't won' but went on to tell how he had reappraised his lifestyle in the wake of the accident to a packed press conference at Addenbrooke's Hospital in Cambridge. 'Right now, the Derby means nothing to me,' he said.

Sitting in a wheelchair, his broken right ankle in a cast, his bloodied forehead stitched, and with heavy bruising to his face and hands, he gave a full account of the horrific details of the accident.

His wife Catherine was among the audience as her husband – at times close to breaking down – told how he had 'stared death in the face' in the crash which occurred as he was leaving Newmarket to fly to the meeting at Goodwood.

And while he might attend Saturday's Vodafone Derby, he hinted that his recovery may, if necessary, stretch beyond the three months it is estimated it will take for his physical injuries to heal.

He said: 'I have no plans to rush myself back into racing. Obviously, racing is the only thing I know and want to do. Physically, bones can be fixed, but there is also the mental aspect of it.

'I hope I can pull through and be strong enough to come back and enjoy what I was doing before this happened.

'Nobody wishes to die, and when it happens very suddenly like that and you have only two seconds to think about it, it's beyond scary. No words can explain that bit.

'It just makes you wonder why we get upset about things. We are forever rushing and chasing our tails, for what?

'It went through my mind to give up, but I'm 29 and what am I going to do? I do love racing very much and I'm planning to do it for another few years.

'Right now, everything feels pretty scary. Once my physical side feels strong, the mental side will follow. But now I feel very vulnerable.

'I stared death in the face. Obviously it wasn't my time and it gives me a completely different approach to life.

'I'm planning to take five minutes more and enjoy the things that I achieve and my family life. It's been a very, very frightening experience.'

Once he gets medical clearance Dettori plans to spend part of his convalescence in Italy with his parents.

But when he is ready to return to race-riding it will be to a career with at least some of the risk taken out as he does not intend to travel by light aircraft in the future.

'We're taking more than everyday risks by flying in bad weather and using short airstrips and grass airstrips. I'm not saying they're not safe, but they leave a bit to the imagination.

'In the past, I even got on fast motorbikes and they felt very dangerous. I've gone a number of different ways and it increases the pressure you put on yourself to get to the top.

'It was a matter of time before an accident like this happened.

'Unfortunately, we lost a pilot and the accident happened to me as well, so I'm not taking that risk anymore.'

'The best therapy has been talking to Ray. We can share emotions, and we're both trying to cheer each other on. He's the guy I've got to turn to for the time being.'

Frankie would not be thirty until just before Christmas. Now we knew just how lucky he was to be with us still. It was a perfect time for David Ashforth to look at the story so far.

When Frankie smiles, the world smiles with him. Not today. Frankie's joyful, infectious smile seems a world away, but it will return – soon, we hope. Crusty old stewards can't stop themselves, Sheikh Mohammed can't stop himself, the solemn face of British racing can't stop itself. Even Lester Piggott smiles when Frankie smiles.

Normal rules of envy don't apply. Dettori's talent and personality shine so bright, and so benevolent, that everyone knows that this is British racing's lucky diamond – its special star to show off proudly to an indifferent world. Our Frankie.

The flying dismount a little tired, the relentless cheeriness a little tiresome; fifteen years in England, and that is the worst a muck-raker can rake up. It's a fruitless dig for dislike. Lanfranco Dettori is a rare celebration. People like him, want to be around him. Racing is fun.

To have emerged so rounded from such a sharp childhood. His father, a poor man from Sardinia, married and soon separated from a circus artist, leaving Lanfranco and his sister, Alessandra, to a half-divorced childhood, while Gianfranco turned himself into Italy's champion jockey, many times.

Born to balance, Frankie fell off Dallas, the quietest horse in Luca Cumani's yard, but learnt quickly, adroit of body and mind. Too young to race-ride in England, at fifteen he returned to Italy to win on Rif. He rode his first British winner on Lizzy Hare at Goodwood in June 1987, aged sixteen, became champion apprentice in 1989, succeeded Ray Cochrane as Cumani's stable jockey and registered his first Group 1 success, on Markofdistinction, in 1990. And wintered in the US.

He put his toes in the stirrups, crouched low, watched the way Chris McCarron and Steve Cauthen changed and rechanged their hands, getting all but the final drop out of a run before picking up their whip. Dettori has fused Europe and America more seamlessly than any other jockey, making it look natural, making it look easy, like he doesn't need to think. But he does think. It is one of his greatest strengths.

In 1993 Dettori thought he would go to Hong Kong, make money and make whoopee, and nothing Cumani said could change his mind. It was changed for him when he accepted a police caution for possession of a small amount of cocaine.

Dettori reacted, as he has always reacted to adversity, by working to get back on track, for, in his life, as in his races, Dettori is mentally strong and disciplined. Light on the surface, but focused, determined, resolute. Loudly applauded, twenty-two, he could have gone the wrong way, but went the right way.

A season that started rockily ended with 149 winners, a partnership with Lochsong, reconciliation with Cumani and a contract to ride for Sheikh Mohammed. No-one knew, when Dettori partnered Dayflower for Satish Seemar in the 1993 One Thousand Guineas, how far that was going to lead.

It led almost immediately to Balanchine – Dettori's, and Godolphin's, first Classic success, celebrated with his natural

showman's ebullience. Racing society, reserved itself, took vicarious pleasure in Dettori's uninhibited displays. His glow softened the Sheikh's public face, ending the notion that the Maktoums didn't smile and, in time, revealing Sheikh Mohammed's own engaging humour.

That autumn, 1994, when the jockey with luck rode the luckless Barathea to win the Breeders' Cup Mile, it was a circle neatly sewn – the debt to Cumani acknowledged and celebrated, the transatlantic link sealed, the Angel Cordero flying dismount launched. An end and a beginning.

Celebrity briefly threatened to divide Dettori's energies, causing a flicker of anxiety in the Godolphin camp, but Dettori is protected from distraction by a fierce liking for success and a dislike of failure.

The best jockeys make the fewest mistakes, and for Dettori they are a rarity. Laughter should not be mistaken for levity. Dettori does his homework, on and off the gallops.

Godolphin regard him as the best judge of a horse in the game, with an intuitive sense of a horse's capabilities. John Gosden regards him as that rarest of creatures – a top jockey and a top work rider combined. Dettori's contribution is to the team, diligently behind the scenes as well as brightly before the cameras.

He prepares and analyses; he rides with calculation and discipline, with a plan. Supremely well balanced, with a gift of timing, rarely where he shouldn't be, transmitting his own inner enthusiasm to the horse, balancing it, cajoling it, knowing the pace and the post, neat and stylish and deceptively strong. Kieren Fallon and Pat Eddery are more obviously effortful, but Dettori, in his different way, extracts all that is there to be given.

Brave, tactically brave. Even Dubai Millennium's facile Dubai World Cup success this spring took courage. It looked as if Dettori may have gone too fast, Dubai Millennium doing too much too soon. He is not afraid to put his neck under the guillotine, a confidence and skill seen to effect on Bachir in the Irish Two Thousand Guineas.

Dettori had also gone into the 1998 Breeders' Cup Classic with a plan – to take Silver Charm, a gritty battler, fast and wide before he could respond. The plan was sound, the execution uncharacteristically inept. Losing his normally calm head, Dettori beat Swain left-handed, relentlessly, sending him right. Then he blamed the lights.

It was the biggest of days, in front of the most critical of audiences, a mistake by a man who doesn't make mistakes, the jockey who, gloriously, had won seven out of seven at Ascot in 1996. It took Dettori a long time, and a lot of thinking, to come to terms with it, even to admit it.

Dettori thrives on success and, when things are going well, he is bursting at the seams. But there is another, introspective side to him, that of a thoughtful man. No criticism is more wounding than a justified one, and Dettori, and his pride, were hurt.

Eventually, he put his head down and got the hands of the clock turning again, not least with Daylami's victory in last year's Breeders' Cup Turf.

Now, Dettori faces another mental and emotional battle. There are a lot of positive things in his life – his wife Catherine, his son, the affection of the friends he himself has been a loyal friend to, sometimes seemingly egotistical but in a kindly way and considerate of others.

The tide of passion and enthusiasm Dettori has brought to racing may be at a low ebb today, but the tide will turn.

FROM THE FLAMES

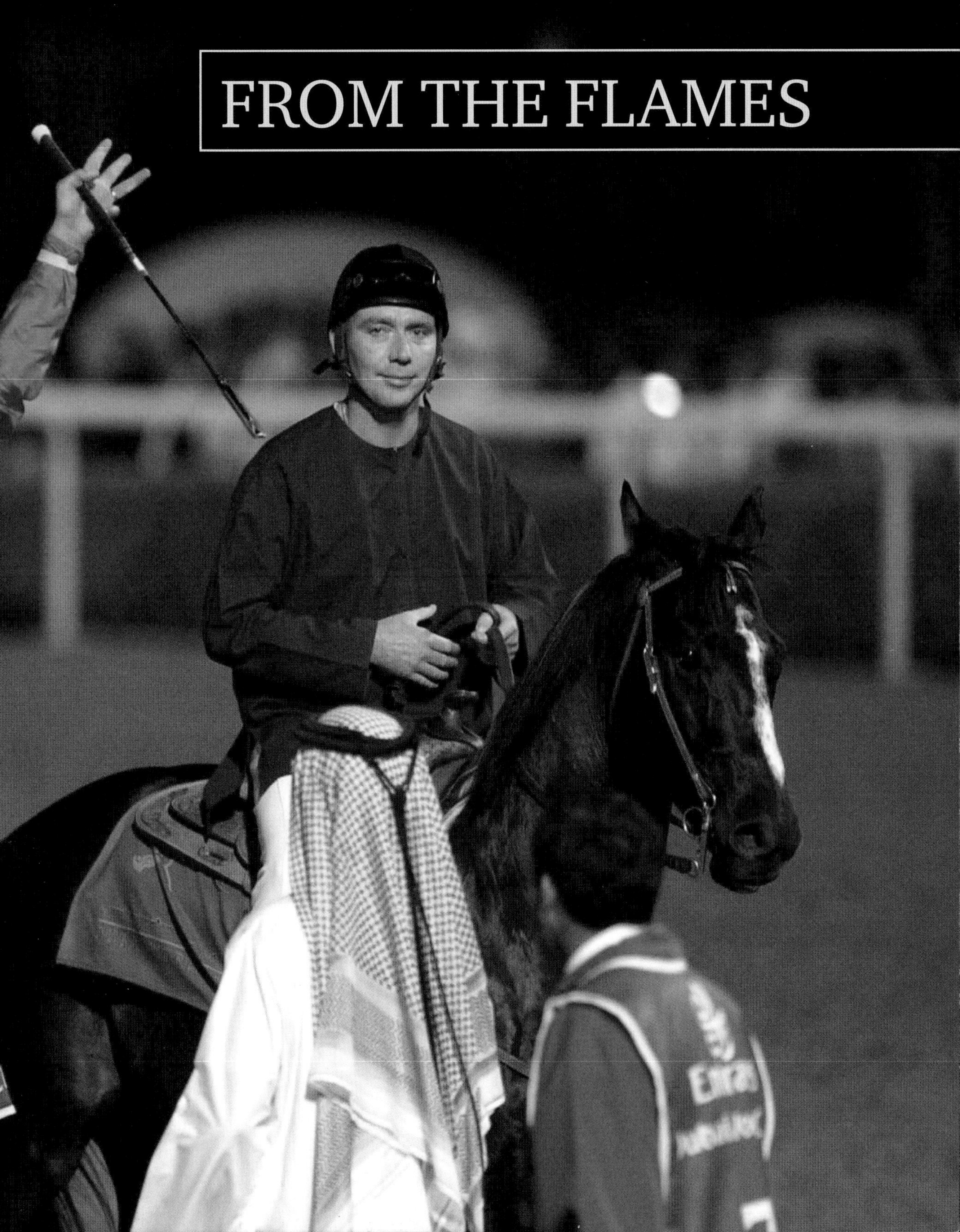

PREVIOUS SPREAD: *Something to celebrate – after Moon Ballad's victory in the 2003 Dubai World Cup.*

OPPOSITE: *Frankie and his beloved Dubai Millennium at Royal Ascot, June 2000.*

*I*t had been as near death as anyone could fear it. The scars were always likely to be as much mental as physical, but for a 29-year-old star athlete in the very prime of his sporting life, pressing on was the obvious recovery path. Yet delivering what he himself called 'this second chance in life' with quite the same obsessive determination as the first time around would not be easy.

For we who had so nearly lost him, the excitement was just the thought of having him back. The first sighting was a last-minute appearance on crutches to watch Dubai Millennium confirm superstar status in the Prince of Wales's Stakes at Royal Ascot, but it was the first ride about which we were all hyperventilating.

It was at the end of July that Tony Elves brought Racing Post *readers the report they had been waiting for.*

Frankie Dettori was back in the saddle yesterday morning for the first time since he was injured in the fatal Newmarket plane crash – and he could return to race-riding next week.

Dettori had originally intended to be back at the York Ebor meeting, which starts on 22 August. However, after riding on the gallops in Newmarket yesterday, he said: 'I could be looking at having my first ride in about ten days' time.'

Dettori, who broke his right ankle in the crash on 1 June, which claimed the life of pilot Patrick Mackey, looked in good health, sporting both a suntan and a beard. His first assignment on the gallops was on the straightforward Zoning, and he admitted: 'It's good to be on a quiet one to start with.'

The Italian's weight rose to 9st 7lb during his absence, but he is now able to ride at 9st, and is raring to get back into the daily swing of morning workouts and race-riding.

'I feel great today and I'll ride out again tomorrow,' he said. 'On the first day you do it on freshness, but the second day hurts and the third day really hurts. After that it's back to normal.

'It's like getting into your car when you come back from holiday. You fiddle around to put the key in the ignition and find out how all the parts work again.'

Dettori reported himself happy with his ankle, saying: 'It's fine – the problem is everything else. Even my fingernails are sore!'

A three-week break in Sardinia appears to have done Godolphin's No.1 jockey the world of good.

'I did a lot of groundwork – walking and swimming – while I was away and it has put a good base on my leg,' Dettori said.

It was a cold, drizzly morning in Newmarket yesterday, and the rider added: 'It's nice to be back, but I wish the weather was a bit better. I used to be tanned before I came to England – then I came here and got white.'

Dettori, who returned to his Stetchworth home on Saturday evening, admitted to having over-indulged during a huge lunch at the Old Plough in Ashley on Sunday afternoon. However, he will now be returning to his more customary dietary habits.

'I had a massive Sunday lunch, but my weight isn't too bad and I'm going back to my normal level now,' he said.

Dettori reported that he has been easily able to flex his slightly scarred right ankle at his home, and he will today see a specialist at Addenbrooke's Hospital, where he was treated following the crash.

'I'm seeing my consultant, and when he sees me I'm sure he'll be delighted,' he added.

When that first race came a fortnight later, it was a unique mix of high performance and poignancy. For a start, it was at the Newmarket July Course, the site of the doomed take-off for that fateful flight in early summer. I remember the sense of expectation in the crowd – and the renewed sense of wonderment when Frankie delivered. Even more than any other of the extraordinary events in his life, it could not have happened but it had.

David Ashforth reported.

Frankie Dettori burst back into the limelight yesterday with a 10-1 double from his two booked rides at Newmarket.

Two months after the plane crash just across the famous Heath which killed his friend and pilot, Patrick Mackey, and which left the Italian with a broken ankle, Dettori could have been excused an element of ring-rustiness.

However, buoyed by a wave of goodwill from the crowd, he gave them what they wanted when driving the 11-4 joint-favourite Atlantis Prince, who had looked beaten when Crazy Larrys loomed upsides a furlong out, to victory by three-quarters of a length in the Tote Exacta Conditions Stakes.

And 35 minutes later he partnered top-weight Dim Sums to victory in the Tote Scoop6 Nursery, in the process landing almost £1.4 million for Scoop6 syndicate 'The Essex Boys'.

Dettori was greeted by rapturous applause on his return to the winner's enclosure after both victories.

'It's a fairytale come true,' he said. 'Two rides and two winners – the first two winners of my new career. People's reactions have been fantastic. It was very emotional.'

There was a subdued, reflective tinge to Dettori's manner at the beginning of the day, and the start of the Tote Exacta Conditions Stakes was not far from the scene of the crash. The rider admitted: 'I got to the start of the first race and tried to collect my thoughts and I just glanced to the wooden huts by the ditch.

'I said, "Hello, ditch", and I froze for a few seconds and my thoughts went to the accident and poor Patrick.'

After Atlantis Prince's victory, he said: 'I thought I was going to be a good second, and had to get serious and everything came back.'

However, he admitted to feeling the pace, as he added later: 'To be honest, I was a little more unfit than I expected. I had done a lot of groundwork and been pushing hard this week.

'The leg felt fine, but I got through the first race on freshness. I was still blowing when I came out for the next, but it opened the pipes and I recovered a lot quicker after the second race. I just hope Catherine isn't feeling randy tonight, as I won't be able to do anything about it!'

If anyone in racing had forgotten Dettori's charismatic qualities and star status, then the day was a stirring, emotional reminder.

When it was announced before racing that he would be appearing in the winner's enclosure at 1.45pm, a crowd no other celebrity in the sport could attract gathered in excited expectation. And he did not disappoint, responding to their warmth with the natural ebullience that is a major part of his popularity.

Louise Corbett and Debbie Eales had travelled from Bedford with a 'Welcome Back' banner and Dettori, characteristically, planted a welcome kiss on Louise's cheek and put his arm around her.

'We were so excited when we heard Frankie would be here,' said Debbie. 'We had to do something for his comeback.'

Nick Lees, Newmarket's racing director, welcomed Dettori back. 'It's wonderful to see you.'

'It's great to be back,' Dettori said. 'I'm very, very excited. It's been a frustrating time. It's nice to be alive. Now we've got to give it a bash.'

But it was to the race fans he spoke, and waved. 'A great thank you, sincerely from my heart,' he said. 'You guys gave me the courage to come back, to do my job. Nothing has given me more pleasure.'

Reporting himself in good shape and down to 8st 7lb, Dettori did, however, warn racegoers not to expect any flying dismounts for a while.

'Fred Robinson, the surgeon, has told me not to be silly and just to slide off gently.' He did.

Then it was kisses to the crowd and an autograph for young Siobhan Jones before the mental challenge of his return to race-riding.

He had openly wondered whether his nerve would be intact, but Ray Cochrane, the other victim of the plane crash, who had also made a successful return, was in no doubt.

He said: 'He'll cope. He's tough and fit and it's a job. You've got to get on with it.'

Last night, Dettori was on his way to Deauville but, in a reminder of the dreadful day that was the origin of his comeback, he said that he would not be flying in a small plane. Instead, he drove to Heathrow to catch a scheduled flight to Paris, before driving to Deauville.

And except on special occasions, he will take Mondays and Tuesdays off, to devote more time to his family.

But yesterday 'his new career' started in the best way possible, and everyone at Newmarket left knowing they had been with a true star.

Afterwards Frankie had a natural winning high and talked of his delight at being back to the camaraderie of the weighing room. But amongst all that and 'lots of ambition to win every race' was a new proviso that he would now 'have to sacrifice my job to give more time to my family. I am planning to enjoy the second time around more than the first time around.'

His head must have been spinning as he then travelled to Normandy for rides next day at Deauville. Our photographer Edward Whitaker shared the journey.

On the plane on Saturday night, Frankie had at first seemed over the moon after his amazing double on his comeback at Newmarket that afternoon. All the way in the car he had been receiving phone calls from his wife Catherine, from the Godolphin team, from his Italian family – 'Bellissimo! Bellissimo!' – English jockeys, French jockeys.

A pensive passenger on Air France.

But now he wanted to tell about the other plane. About the flight that fell. About the miracles that saved him.

We were travelling to Deauville for his ride on Lend A Hand in yesterday's Prix Maurice de Gheest. After the tragic air crash on 1 June, he says he will never fly on a small plane again.

That makes Newmarket to Normandy an eight-hour car-and-Heathrow journey, rather than a one-hour flight. I was taken along for company.

Over the years, I have photographed Frankie hundreds of times: as a teenage apprentice, on Lochsong in the Nunthorpe, on Barathea in the Breeders' Cup, on Lammtarra in the Arc, on the Swain disaster, on the Daylami redemption.

And this year I had lensed Dubai Millennium's Dubai World Cup procession and, much more darkly, had the unhappy duty of recording Frankie and other mourners at the funeral of pilot Patrick Mackey.

Saturday morning had, of course, started with the bad news of Dubai Millennium [who had broken a leg on the Newmarket gallops]. 'I was on the running machine in my sweat gear,' said Frankie as the car sped southwards.

'When the call came through that Dubai Millennium had broken down I went out to Catherine, who was playing in the garden with Leo, and I just said the three words, "He broke down", and walked back in.

'I was gutted. I looked at the machine and said, "Stuff it, I can't be bothered to come back." It took half an hour to pull myself together. But we were lucky. It could have happened in the match [the proposed match race against Montjeu]. That could have been fatal to him. And to me.'

But by the time Frankie reached the racecourse he was back in his most positive of moods. Characteristically, he had Catherine and Leo, his mother and father-in-law and surgeon Fred Robinson with him as support.

'It was out of this world,' he said. 'I revel in the occasion. Racing needs me and I need racing. Everyone was wonderful, but I was still nervous as to how I would be on the horse.'

The facts say that Atlantis Prince won by three quarters of a length, but for Frankie there was much more to it than that. 'Two furlongs out the other horse went a length ahead and then suddenly it all came back,' he remembered as we closed on Heathrow. 'I pumped and pushed and threw everything at him. The other horse began to weaken and I began to edge ahead. Everything was working again.

'The way I ride,' he explained, 'is to handle the horse like a ball of energy. The horse doesn't know how far he has to run. I have to distribute the energy throughout the trip to maximize the potential of the horse. It is all down to feeling and timing.

'The really wonderful thing about Saturday is that, for a while, I thought I was going to be second, but then that old feeling took over, and I just had to win.'

We are at Heathrow. Well-wishers are everywhere. A man from Alitalia comes up, to whose daughter Frankie is godfather. We are going Air France to Charles de Gaulle. The flight is easy, but Frankie starts to remember that dreadful first day of June.

'It wasn't a normal day,' he said, looking out of the window at a beautiful August sunset. 'It was horrible. Every colour was grey. Now I look back on the crash, there is definitely a God.

'Whenever there was a plane journey to the races Richard Hills would phone me up. That day he didn't, so I rang him to offer a lift to Goodwood. Richard said he had already left as he had to pick up some lobsters from Chichester.

'If Richard had been on the plane we would have been facing each other in the crash. Our faces would have smashed. One or both of us would have died.

'So there was only Ray and me sitting with empty seats in front of us. That was the first of the miracles.

'Ray had been studying for his pilot's licence and when we took off he knew at once that we were in trouble. That Patrick was in difficulty with one engine. Somehow, Patrick avoided the bank. He saved our lives. I was praying.

'There was this terrible feeling of falling. You clutched the seats, tensed muscles you didn't know you had. But while the body was tense, the mind relaxed. That was it. You were just waiting to die. Thinking about pieces of metal ripping your body. Of legs being chopped off. When we hit the ground. I closed my eyes. No words can describe the power of hitting the ground.

'The first thing I remember when I came to in the plane is staring at the horizon like a film with a 180-degree panorama. I couldn't move or speak, but I wanted to.

'That moment felt like ten minutes. I saw the pilot, the grey day, the bank, the left engine burning like a house fire. I didn't know if I was in the real world. It could have been ten seconds or ten minutes. It was like a 45rpm record being played at 33. And then it sped up, like a 78.

'Then Ray said the plane was going to explode. He shouted to get out. I was closest to the door, but it had crumpled on landing and we couldn't get out that way. But the luggage door, which could only be opened from the outside, was half-open. What kind of miracle is that?

'When we got out of the plane I was in pain, shock and disbelief. I didn't know what had happened. Only then did I feel the pain. The leg was hurting unbelievably. There was so much blood. It was caked all over my face. I thought I'd lost my right eye. Then Ray dragged me away from the flames to safety.

'Sitting on the grass, I saw Ray going back to try to rescue the pilot. Beating the flames with his jacket, screaming like a madman. Then the plane started to explode into little balls of fire.

'When I left the plane I could see Patrick with his head slumped. I thought he was dead already. I was worried about Ray near the plane. When Ray couldn't get to the pilot he threw himself on the ground, screaming. Then Ray came up to me going mental, shouting, "He saved our lives! He saved our lives." Me and Ray had a hug and a cry. Ray dialled 999 on his mobile.'

Sitting beside Frankie above the clouds on Saturday evening was to feel the emotion, the intensity of the recollection and the sympathy of the man. But later, on the long car drive to Deauville, he came down to earth as he reflected on Dubai Millennium, the best horse he ever rode.

'He was a monster,' said Frankie. 'He was the horse who was going to destroy the Americans. He would finally put the Swain thing to rest. I can't tell you how much that hurt me. It hurts me still. Now Dubai Millennium can't run. But at least he's saved.'

So, too, is Frankie. And he intends to make the best of what he calls 'This second time around'.

Even during this drive he is constantly on the phone to his family and friends, especially to Catherine and to Leo, his 'little monkey'.

This is a man passionate about the good things in life. 'I love good food, fine wines, coming to Deauville and all that,' he says. 'Some jockeys get depressed by it all. But I like to exercise hard so that I can eat.'

One of the phone calls has been to Olivier Peslier. We meet him at La Guinguette and start the most delicious of seafood meals.

'Yes,' said Frankie, 'I have been blessed.'

The blessings at the highest racing level were resumed when Frankie returned to Deauville and landed his first Group 1 success since the crash when Godolphin's Muhtathir landed the Prix Jacques le Marois at Deauville. Concerns about his ankle prevented the usual flying dismount celebration, but this was resumed when Crystal Music won the Fillies' Mile at Ascot at the end of September – albeit a table top version that had been tested a few days earlier when Frankie was a guest on the Michael Parkinson television show, something repeated in the equally non-racing environment of the Oxford Union a month later.

His season was to close out in overseas triumph when Fantastic Light won the Hong Kong Cup at Sha Tin in December, and his achievements were given royal recognition with an MBE in the New Year's Honours List. But in early November, at Churchill Downs in Kentucky for the Breeders' Cup, he told the Racing Post's *Jon Lees that he had recognized how close had been his call, as he paid tribute to his friend Ray Cochrane.*

Frankie Dettori yesterday admitted that both he and Ray Cochrane returned to the saddle too early in an attempt to put the horrific experience of their air crash ordeal behind them.

Muhtathir after winning at Deauville.

Fantastic Light wins the Hong Kong Cup from Greek Dance, December 2000.

Five months after the fatal accident, Dettori is back at his peak, ready to add to his international race record with four rides at the Breeders' Cup.

But following Cochrane's decision to retire earlier this week, Dettori conceded that with hindsight he should have given himself more time to get over the mental and physical scars.

'We both made the same mistake,' he said, speaking at Churchill Downs in Louisville after riding work.

'We came back too early because we wanted to get the bad memories out of our minds and make sure we got back to the track and got on with our lives.

'I went through hell and back to get back. It took me eight weeks with a broken ankle and I did it just for Dubai Millennium and he should have been here now.

Frankie receives his MBE from Foreign Secretary – and racing fanatic – the late Robin Cook.

'Unfortunately the day I came back, he broke his leg. But I was committed to coming back, so I had to go through with it and I found I wasn't really mentally or physically ready.

'I had to stop-start the first month and then I got back into my routine.

'I did take my time and tried to take a few days off here and there, but once I was committed I couldn't turn back. The Godolphin team was screaming for me to stay on because up to then we didn't have such a great time.'

Dettori paid tribute to Cochrane, who had not only saved his life by dragging him away from the burning plane, but had provided valuable advice during his rise to the top.

He added: 'We go back a long way because when I first started with Luca Cumani as an apprentice, he came as first jockey. He taught me a lot and he also pulled me to safety from the plane crash. I owe him a lot.

'I'm very pleased he decided to call it a day. At least he got out of the game in one piece.'

Within days Frankie had made Ray Cochrane his agent. Andrew Stringer had taken over on Matty Cowing's retirement, but the ties with Ray were much too strong, even if the needs of rest and recovery from the removal of the screws in the right ankle meant that there were no rides to book until a winning comeback in the Maktoum Challenge at Nad al Sheba in Dubai in February 2001.

The break was not without its diversions, including a week at the end of January when Frankie both officially opened a new £2.4 million development at Addenbrooke's and did best man duties at the wedding of his old stablemate Colin Rate at Newmarket. In March his family happiness was augmented by the birth of daughter Ella, but for Godolphin a traditional slow start to the British season was compounded by the bitterest of Racing Post *stories on the first day of May.*

Dubai Millennium, the £30 million horse hailed by Sheikh Mohammed as the best to run under the Godolphin banner, died on Sunday night after losing his battle with the mystery disease grass sickness.

Frankie Dettori said: 'He was the ultimate racehorse – the thing that everyone who breeds or trains or rides dreams about being associated with – so this is a very sad day. We always knew he was going to be a champion, right from day one, and he proved it.

'I don't think any of us involved with him will ever forget his performances in the Dubai World Cup or at Royal Ascot. They were truly awesome.

'You'd have to go back to the days of Ribot to find anything to compare with those wins, and I'm proud to think that I'm always going to be able to say I was a part of the team.

'Dubai Millennium was one of the great racehorses – the best I have ever ridden and probably the best I will ever ride – and his death is a huge loss for racing. He meant so much to Darley Stud, to Sheikh Mohammed, and to me.'

Godolphin may have started slowly, but the big races for them and for Frankie soon began to come. Fantastic Light won the Tattersalls Gold Cup at the Curragh and then the Prince of Wales's Stakes as part of a Dettori treble on the second day of Royal Ascot. The Ed Dunlop-trained Lailani won the Irish Oaks and the Nassau Stakes under Britain's favourite Italian, Noverre won the Sussex Stakes and Sakhee was hugely impressive in the Juddmonte International at York. But for satisfaction nothing beat Fantastic Light's Irish Champion Stakes victory over his King George conqueror Galileo in a 'go for home early' plot hatched by Sheikh Maktoum and Sheikh Mohammed in front of a disbelieving Dettori on the eve of the race.

Receiving the Ritz Club Trophy from HM The Queen Mother at Ascot, June 2001.

Fantastic Light in the King George, 2001, in which he finished runner-up to Gallileo.

Fantastic Light was to close out his 'annus mirabilis' with a Breeders' Cup Turf victory at Belmont Park, but before that Frankie had taken his Group 1 tally to 100 in the finest fashion by storming away with the Prix de l'Arc de Triomphe at Longchamp. In Britain he may have ridden 'only' 94 winners, but worldwide it had been a year to remember, as Matt Chapman wrote.

Frankie Dettori yesterday reflected on his 'best-ever season' and predicted that the outstanding forces of European racing – Godolphin and Coolmore – will grow ever stronger due to their 'healthy rivalry'.

Britain's racing superstar is looking forward to a winter of travel, holiday and work in which he will jet from Mauritius to Hong Kong, and from Italy to Dubai.

Yesterday he looked back at a 'fantastic' Flat season, with the highlights being Fantastic Light's Breeders' Cup Turf success and Sakhee's Prix de l'Arc de Triomphe victory.

Dettori said: 'It has been my best-ever season. I've had seventeen Group 1 winners – that's if you include the one I had in Singapore – and it would have been eighteen if Noverre hadn't been disqualified after winning the French Guineas.

'In particular, I've been lucky enough to ride two great horses in Fantastic Light and Sakhee. To get one would have been amazing, but to have two in one season was incredible.'

Although Godolphin's three-year-olds were a far from vintage crop, the older horses more than made up for it and ended up flying the blue flag with distinction.

'It didn't look good at the start of the season – but we came through in the end,' Dettori added.

Reflecting on the Godolphin–Coolmore rivalry, Dettori said: 'Coolmore have been very good for us – they make us get better and we do the same for them.

'It is a nice, healthy rivalry which can only make both teams stronger. Without Godolphin and Coolmore there would be so much less interest.

'That said, don't forget there are other major owners. The Aga Khan has had a quiet year, but he cleaned up last season. All you need is just one good horse.'

Coolmore have proved invincible, with trainer Aidan O'Brien gathering 23 Group or Grade 1 wins this year, and Dettori added: 'They have been outstanding with their two-year-olds and we have to try hard to keep up.

'Galileo, though, was nothing until he won the Derby – he had struggled in his trial – so you never know which horse will come through.

'David Loder has had about five two-year-olds that have really excited me, and of course Dubai Destination is one of them.

After the Arc – Sakhee returns.

'He's had an injury, but I'm hoping he'll come back. I don't like talking up these horses too much, though, as I always put a jinx on them!'

Looking forward to the winter, Dettori added: 'I've always wanted to go to Mauritius – people tell me it's beautiful – so I'm looking forward to riding there. My father has been and he says it's wonderful.

'Before that I'm not going to Japan now that Fantastic Light has been retired, but I will be off to Hong Kong. I will then take a holiday and then it's Dubai. I just hope next year is as good as this one.'

It was not to be. Sure, Kazzia and Frankie won the One Thousand Guineas and Oaks, Grandera was a brilliantly ridden winner of the Irish Champion Stakes and Marienbard a surprise victor of the Arc under Frankie for Godolphin, but throughout the year negative pressures would not go away. In the racing world there was the sadness of the death of Matty Cowing in June, but in the wider world there was the distracting announcement that Frankie was to succeed John Parrott as one of the captains of BBC Television's A Question of Sport *– this following his endorsements of everything from ice cream to pizza and appearances on the likes of* Top of the Pops *and* TFI Friday.

Over a long career, Racing Post *writer Howard Wright thought he had seen it all. As he discovered in August 2002, he was wrong.*

Frankie Dettori is preparing a pasta lunch. He has worked four horses for Godolphin, including Grandera and Marienbard, played nine holes of golf, and made a quick trip to Waitrose. He is now using his skills in the kitchen of the family home on the outskirts of Newmarket, while daily helpers Libby and Lucy match strides with the effervescent Dettori youngsters, Leo and Ella. Wife Catherine is in London for the day.

It's a Thursday. Dettori is not on the racecourse, and *At The Races* is playing to an audience of none on a huge television in the lounge area.

The scenario explains why some critics have questioned Dettori's appetite for his day job.

Into the winner's enclosure after winning the One Thousand Guineas on Kazzia.

They have said he spends too many midweek afternoons away from the office, and is in danger of dulling the cutting edge that brought him a double century of winners, and the jockeys' championship, in 1994 and 1995.

This year he will struggle to beat the 75 winners he rode in Britain as champion apprentice in 1989, despite a twenty per cent strike rate.

Dettori is aware of the criticism and admits it hurts.

He says: 'I know that for some people I'm either brilliant or no good; there's no in-between.

'The press got my back up this year, especially because Godolphin had a bad start. I'm stubborn and pretty thick-skinned, but I'm like any normal human being, and it hurts to read that you're not giving it your best shot. Of course I am, but in a different way. Because I don't go to the smaller meetings any more, it doesn't mean I don't care.'

As he prepares to turn 32 in December, with a young family, and obviously influenced by the plane crash two years ago, Dettori remains assured about his motives, and his ability.

He says: 'I want to win more than anybody else, and I'm probably more hungry than I've ever been, because I'm doing it for a different purpose. Before, I did it for ego, self-esteem, for myself. Now I've got a wife and family to think about, and I'm doing it for them, so the pressure is probably greater.

'But to get myself to another level, I've sacrificed pounding away every day. After what I've been through, and what I've got in terms of the job with Godolphin, there's no sense in spending five hours going up and down the motorway just to ride one more winner.

'Doing that day in and day out does jeopardise your hunger. You get to the middle of the season and say to yourself, "Who am I doing this for, the man in the betting shop or myself?" My hunger is now channelled in a different way. It's working, and I'm bringing in the results. And I've felt a lot happier in the last year.

'I know I can fly 25 hours to Melbourne next month and arrive there as if the season has just started. I won't go there worn out from riding 900 races.'

Ferrari Frankie

The career change began for Dettori when the Godolphin operation started to grow, but it was compounded by the events of June 2000, which claimed the life of pilot Patrick Mackey, and from which he was rescued by his now-agent Ray Cochrane.

Dettori reasons: 'You have to do one thing or the other - either be champion jockey or concentrate on the bigger meetings.

'John Gosden has left Newmarket [to train at Manton, though he later returned to Newmarket], David Loder has a different approach these days, and Godolphin have only fifty horses. Plus I'm away in Europe most Sundays and have to leave in the middle of October to ride in Japan and so forth.

'I'd have to be well in front by this time of year to be champion jockey, which is most unlikely. It would be like giving six weeks' start to Kieren Fallon. In my heart of hearts I'd love to have one more crack at the championship – for self-esteem, so I could turn round and say "Up yours!" to those people who've given me a hard time.

'Sure, I've thought about it, because I'm very ambitious, but in the circumstances I can't do it.'

Dettori gives short shrift to criticism that his new approach risks leaving him short of match practice.

'I ride work three times a week, and walk or run 5km six days a week. I'm in great shape physically and mentally, and when you're working with horses, you either have the sixth sense to understand them straight away and find the key, or you haven't.

'I feel more in control than ever. I'm not in a routine, like many other jockeys. I'm more alert and see the whole picture clearer, because I'm not stuffed by riding too much and travelling too much. I have more time to think and study, and take things in.'

While the approach might have changed, Dettori remains true to character – stubborn, opinionated and the racing personality with the highest profile outside the sport.

He says: 'The way I've operated and done the job in the past has been successful, so you have to be opinionated, though you still have to keep your ears open and look for improvement. But you have to be stubborn, and at the end of the day I have to do what I think is best.

'It's black and white for ninety per cent of the time, but the other ten per cent depends on you being self-confident enough to keep one step ahead. That can be very risky. You can never get ten out of ten right, but if you have enough confidence to get, say, seven out of ten, that's okay.

'No sportsman in the world can be 100 per cent all the time. Even at eighty per cent, I'd still be riding well. My worst isn't bad – it's as good as anybody else – but it wouldn't be the Frankie Dettori you'll see on Arc day.

'It's hard to get this across, but I can't be Magnificent Seven every Saturday. At least I got there once!'

Dettori accepts there is huge responsibility in riding for the Godolphin team.

'There's the trainer, Saeed bin Suroor, and the racing manager, Simon Crisford, and we're all on the same wavelength. Though we argue every day – and I'm the first to stir the pot –we have the same game plan when we go into battle.

'It's a privilege to work for Sheikh Mohammed, but there's pressure, because he's the best loser in the world. It's a sort of reverse psychology. When someone is so understanding, you automatically double the pressure, because you want to do so well for him. When that happens, you can go to a level you don't know you've got.'

He recalls the Irish Champion Stakes this month, when Grandera collared Hawk Wing virtually on the line, as a perfect example.

'When I watch the video, it shocks me. I look at it and say, "That's not me, it must be somebody else."

'I have to say thanks to the Godolphin team, because everybody put so much into the race. If we hadn't supplemented Best Of The Bests, we wouldn't have won.

'Hawk Wing has only one style of running. He can follow anything and outsprint them. But if you give him two horses, you've got him in the middle.

'If he gives too much ground to the one in front, like Best Of The Bests, he won't catch him, but if he goes after him, he'll set it up for Grandera.

'It worked, and we nearly had first and second, though at one stage Grandera didn't want to go, and I was hoping we'd win with Best Of The Bests.

'I said I wouldn't move until Mick Kinane did on Hawk Wing. He judged it to the last half a metre, but Grandera got there just in time.'

Dettori warms to the occasion from his armchair. 'I love the big day, and the big stage.'

Protest though he might, logical though his 'keep yourself for the big race' strategy may have seemed, the reality was that parts of the racing world were beginning to lose faith in him. The UK 2002 totals of 69 winners and £1.9 million in earnings were his lowest in twenty years, barring the plane crash-punctured season of 2000. Frankie may have shed tears of patriotic joy when the Italian-trained Falbrav won the Japan Cup in November 2002 and Moon Ballad may have produced a career-topping run in the Dubai World Cup in March 2003, but when in April British racegoers were treated to a Dettori head first dyed blond for a TV reality show and then shaven-headed to remove traces of it, it was hardly surprising that the mutterings increased.

Frankie Dye-tori!

A brilliant ride on Dubai Destination on the first day of Royal Ascot, a first Classic for veteran trainer Paddy Mullins in the Irish Oaks with Vintage Tipple, and Godolphin's 100th Group 1 with Sulamani in the Arlington Million may have been individual achievements but it was not until someone on A Question of Sport *had asked, 'When did you retire' that the penny fully dropped.*

That autumn there were European Group 1s for Godolphin with Mezzo Soprano in the Prix Vermeille and with Mamool in the Preis von Europa, but it was the circumstances surrounding a minor race at Lingfield in November which best identified a still unspoken change of direction. Geoff Lester was there.

Frankie Dettori, who sidestepped his 'annual booze-up' at the Cartier Awards on Wednesday night, clinched his tenth century of winners when winning on Rendezvous Point at Lingfield yesterday.

Dettori, delighted to bring up the ton on his old pal John Gosden's filly, thrilled the sparse crowd with his customary flying leap from the saddle and then proceeded to spray his celebratory bottle of champagne into the assembled racegoers, Grand Prix style.

It was Dettori's first 100 since 1999, and the relief at being able to finish off his domestic season on the Polytrack rather than face the horrendous kickback of Wolverhampton's fibresand was all too evident.

'The breaks between the tons were due to the plane crash I suffered and several other things, but it is good to get there again. It has not been a vintage year, but we have finished with a bit of a flourish.

'I could not have hoped for a better start to the year, winning two Group 1s in Dubai in March, including the World Cup on Moon Ballad, but we slipped down a few snakes in midsummer and that was disappointing.

'With Godolphin having only nine Group 1 winners this year things have not gone as well as we would have liked, but I won an Irish Oaks for Paddy Mullins and the likes of Mamool and [Cheveley Park Stakes winner] Carry On Katie got us out of jail at the back end.

'When John [Gosden] told me that he was coming I knew that he must fancy Rendezvous Point, so I declined my invitation for the Cartier Awards in London last night.

'With this filly in the 12.20 I didn't fancy coming straight from Annabel's!'

Dettori, who has booked rides in Rome on Sunday, flies out to Dubai with his wife Catherine and two of their four children next Tuesday for a holiday, but he will return to Britain before heading to Hong Kong for the International races in December.

He added: 'I am so glad that I reached the hundred here, as I didn't fancy having to flog up to Wolverhampton on Monday – now I can relax with Tallula, our new-born baby girl.'

Getting close up and personal with one of Royal Ascot's historic Greencoats.

Frankie closed out 2003 with a splendid triumph on the massive Falbrav in Hong Kong for his old mentor Luca Cumani, and by the time he was ready to re-start in Britain in March 2004 his intentions were becoming clear.

Tony Elves filed the story.

Frankie Dettori is likely to be seen on a more regular basis during the Flat turf season that kicks off this month.

Dettori will be back in England for the Winter Derby at Lingfield tomorrow week, but his absence on Mondays is likely to be a thing of the past as his enthusiasm appears stronger than ever.

Although he has not set his sights on adding to the championships he took in 1994 and 1995 with totals of 233 and 211 winners respectively, the nation's best-known jockey will be wooing his public more frequently.

Dettori said yesterday: 'I will be riding a lot more Godolphin horses now they are moving into Stanley House. There will be at least double the horses they had last season, which means a lot of extra rides.

'I am also going to try to help out Jeremy Noseda and John Gosden when I can, and I will be back in England on a full-time basis after the Dubai World Cup.'

Greeted by Luca Cumani after landing the Hong Kong Cup, December 2003.

A treble on that first day at Lingfield was a perfect setting of the tone. A five-timer at Folkestone in April led the Racing Post's *Lee Mottershead to write about 'a revitalized and rampant Frankie Dettori', and a flood of money for him becoming champion jockey. Later in the year he was to tell the* Guardian *'the turning point came when my wife Catherine made me look at the truth. After the plane crash I kept telling myself there's more to life than being a jockey. I wanted to be this family man who did some nice safe work on the telly.' Now he was back on the championship trail, and even helping Catherine to open and close her riding career with victory in a charity race at Newbury in the week before Ascot in June.*

He was leading jockey at the Royal Meeting for the fifth time with six winners, including Refuse To Bend in the Queen Anne Stakes, Papineau

in the Gold Cup and Doyen a record-breaker in the Hardwicke. Lee Mottershead again:

In a week of Godolphin firsts, this was over in a second.

At the end of a Royal Ascot where Sheikh Mohammed's team have run rampant, they saved the best till last. And the best could just be one of the best that Godolphin have ever had.

Always cantering through a frenetically run Hardwicke Stakes, Doyen cruised into the lead just past the quarter-mile pole.

When he quickened, he left the already sizzling turf scorched. In the blinking of an eyelid, Doyen had stormed lengths clear, six at the line, the Sadler's Wells colt careering away from high-class opponents.

At a place where regal carriages have adorned the track all week, this was the most majestic procession of them all.

'I'm speechless,' said Frankie Dettori, which you don't hear very often.

Yet Dettori was entitled to be. Ascot's mile-and-a-half track record had been held by Stanerra since 1983.

Completing the Hardwicke course – on admittedly firm ground – in 2min 26.53sec, Doyen smashed 0.42sec, or about two lengths, off the previous best.

Dettori said: 'He reminds me of the good old days with Swain and Daylami.

'If Sulamani, Papineau and Doyen turned up for the King George, I don't know which I'd ride. Sulamani loves a bit of cut, and I've ridden Doyen twice on firm and he seems to love it.'

These were the best of times, and good winners kept coming. Refuse To Bend won the Eclipse and Doyen the King George VI and Queen Elizabeth Diamond Stakes. At York, Sulamani landed the Juddmonte International and Rule Of Law the Voltigeur, while Dubai Millennium's best son Dubawi took the National Stakes at the Curragh. But it was the battle for the jockeys' championship that caught the public imagination.

Frankie had actually led the race back in April and again at the beginning of August. By the end of that month Kieren Fallon was eleven winners ahead, only for Frankie to storm on and sit eighteen winners clear by 23 October and being able to travel over to ride Wilko to a shock 28-1 win in the Breeders' Cup Juvenile at Lone Star Park in Texas – after which he returned to the champagne-spraying celebrations at Doncaster in November.

Beforehand Michael Caulfield, chief executive of the Jockeys' Association before becoming a leading sports psychiatrist, had a unique take on what Frankie had done.

When Frankie Dettori is crowned champion jockey on Saturday, he will justifiably be proud of his achievement. Forget the monetary rewards, the new best-selling autobiography or the media interest in his success, this is all about inner satisfaction. This may not be in the Ali category of regaining a title, but it is still a great achievement.

Frankie will be in that glorious position of being able to look himself in the mirror knowing that he honoured the commitments he laid out for himself at the start of the season.

Frankie's farewell to the 'old' Ascot before the rebuilding, 2004.

His season has been free of excuses and distractions. Even when he had the occasional setback, such as the broken finger at Goodwood, he came back with the same attitude.

Not only has his riding been a pleasure to watch, so has his reaction to victory and defeat. He has cherished the triumphs and been magnanimous in defeat. His enthusiasm for work and winning seems to have rubbed off on those around him. From a distance, the Godolphin team enjoyed being part of the success and seemed to feel obliged to keep providing him with winners. Everyone got dragged into the championship quest and that created further momentum.

Of course Frankie had the firepower and support to launch a title challenge, but that would be doing him a disservice. The fact that

Wilko wins the Breeders' Cup Juvenile at Lone Star Park, Texas, in 2004.

Champion jockey en famille *at Doncaster, November 2004*

he has ridden nearly 120 'outside' winners illustrates his renewed commitment to riding.

From the moment he announced his intention to ride 150 winners, he knew he was back in business. The early-season five-timer at Folkestone indicated that his attitude and mindset were different from past years.

Frankie's achievement is a lesson to all top-class athletes who strive to reach and stay at the top of their profession. For all the rewards sport offers, the most satisfaction will always come from actually competing and winning. If that is the first and only priority, then the rest will follow accordingly.

This was the season when Frankie didn't wait for the good days to arrive. He went out and ensured that every day became meaningful. He kept the momentum going throughout the year and the seemingly impossible became possible. All the momentum, confidence and

self-belief were evident when riding Wilko to victory at the Breeders'
Cup. That ride summed up his year.

He can enjoy his winter break satisfied that he gave absolutely
everything in 2004. Even if he doesn't repeat the feat next season,
as long as he keeps setting himself ambitious targets and commits
himself to riding every day, he will be maximizing his extraordinary
talent.

*Firebreak lands the Hong Kong Mile,
December 2004.*

THE UNCLIMBED PEAK

PREVIOUS SPREAD: *Ramonti (no. 6) short-heads Jeremy (near side) to win the Queen Anne Stakes at Royal Ascot, June 2007.*

A year which started with having a race meeting held in his honour in Sicily, receiving the Flat Jockey of The Year award at The Lesters, and being invited to dine with the Queen always had the potential for anticlimax – and that's not casting any aspersions on the arrival of Rocco Dettori, Frankie and Catherine's fifth child, in January 2005.

In 2005 there were early victories for Shamardal in the French Guineas and French Derby, but although Dubawi overcame Newmarket disappointment to win the Irish Two Thousand Guineas he failed to stay in the Derby, and Frankie then had to miss the whole of Royal Ascot (moved that year to York) through suspension following a careless riding charge. Much worse was to follow, as Rodney Masters described in early July.

Frankie Dettori yesterday announced that his fight was over to retain the crown of champion jockey, and claimed that any one of three of his rivals could take over the mantle.

The stricken jockey said he was hurting like never before after a racing accident following a crashing fall at Sandown on Saturday that is set to put him on the sidelines for at least four weeks.

Mwah! A smacker for the eponymous Lester.

Dubawi wins the Irish Two Thousand Guineas, May 2005

Although finding it painful to breathe, the discomfort failed to prevent Dettori expressing an opinion on the battle for a jockeys' championship he's convinced is now out of his reach.

'I know the championship has gone,' Dettori told the *Racing Post*. 'Already I've readjusted my target for the season, which now is to ride 100 winners.'

In his absence, Dettori believes the title race will shape into a three-way battle between Jamie Spencer, the new favourite, Richard Hughes and Robert Winston.

Speaking in little more than a whisper, Dettori said: 'I know Jamie is hot favourite, but I believe it's likely to prove close between the three of them, and Seb Sanders may well enter the equation when Sir Mark Prescott's horses hit top form, which can be any day now.'

He added: 'I'd more or less ruled myself out of contention before Saturday because my stable hasn't peaked in the same way that it did last year.

'Until I've undergone surgery it'll be impossible to state with any accuracy when I'll be fit to return, but I'll be pleasantly surprised if it's less than a month. On the plus side, us jockeys are very fit and as a result we tend to mend well, so it shouldn't be too long.'

Dettori saw a specialist yesterday morning and will undergo surgery in Cambridge tomorrow to plate the left collarbone he fractured in a high-speed spinning fall.

'I appreciate the consequences of my fall could have been far more serious, so although right now I'm hurting more than I've ever done – apart from the fracture there's also plenty of bruising – I'm also reflecting on how fortunate I've been.'

He recalls every second of the incident when sprinter Celtic Mill crashed without warning.

'He clipped the heels of Darryll's horse, and instantly I knew I was in for a big one. A five-furlong sprint on fast ground, and it's a miracle if you walk away unhurt.

'I've had quite a few falls over the years, but I've never hit the ground so hard. Fortunately, I kept rolling. I heard Celtic Mill behind me. The sound was obviously of him rolling, too. I thought he'd come over and squash me. I was waiting for it to happen. Under the circumstances, we were incredibly fortunate to get away with it. I'm thrilled he's all right.'

After X-rays at Kingston General Hospital, he was driven home.

'Every time the car bumped over a cat's eye it hurt all over. By the time we got back to Newmarket I'd taken so many painkillers I didn't really know what I was looking at when I put in the video to watch the fall again. Not that I needed to watch it.

'I spent the night by myself on the couch in the lounge and slept surprisingly well once I found a comfortable position. However, I woke up feeling sore all over, probably more sore than I've ever been in my life, and it does hurt to breathe. I went to see my specialist, and he organised surgery for Tuesday.'

Dettori has won three Classics this season, two in France and one in Ireland, but on the domestic front his season has failed to strike a constant rhythm.

He missed the entire Royal Ascot at York meeting after picking up a six-day careless riding suspension when deemed responsible for a collision at Haydock.

Frankie overdid his haste to recover in time to ride Dubawi in what proved to be a brilliant victory for Godolphin's second jockey Kerrin McEvoy. He was not able to resume until the end of August, and by the close of the next month had taken two decisions which were to have far-reaching consequences. In the Queen Elizabeth II Stakes at Newmarket (transferred from Ascot), he would ignore Sheikh Mohammed's instructions in defeat on Dubawi, while in the St Leger a fortnight earlier he had taken the winning ride from the Sheikh's greatest rivals. Lee Mottershead had the story.

It was, as Frankie Dettori admitted, 'weird'. True, this was Coolmore's day of days, but it did not come to pass without a little help from their friends at Godolphin.

With Shamardal after winning the Prix du Jockey Club, 2005.

Frankie wins the 2005 St Leger on Scorpion in the colours of the Coolmore operation – Godolphin's major rivals.

For yesterday at Doncaster, Dettori swapped one set of superpower silks for another and salvaged a soggy Ladbrokes St Leger with a dramatic all-the-way win aboard odds-on favourite Scorpion.

The sight of Sheikh Mohammed's pride and joy Dettori sporting the colours of Godolphin's fiercest rival was strange. Strange but wholly effective. The way Dettori dictated the pace on Scorpion before nursing his mount to success emphasised why Aidan O'Brien had swooped for the champion jockey's services.

O'Brien got his man, and just thirty minutes before Oratorio added to his 2003 St Leger–Irish Champion double by winning at Leopardstown, he and Dettori enjoyed their first victory together and their third individual St Leger wins.

'It's weird,' said Dettori, who on Tuesday passed up the chance to ride Motivator in Ireland.

'We knew that Motivator was fifty-fifty to run on Tuesday and I knew that this horse was going spare. Aidan wanted an answer, so I went for Scorpion.

'I've got to say thanks to Sheikh Mohammed for letting me ride the horse and also thanks to Coolmore. I've got mixed emotions as I usually win these races for Godolphin and Sheikh Mohammed.'

While the afternoon belonged to Coolmore, Ballydoyle and O'Brien, at Doncaster it was all about Dettori.

As he and Scorpion circled the paddock before the race, so many of those who surrounded the enclosure were shouting his name.

After the race, they cheered him again as he returned to the winner's enclosure throwing kisses to the crowd before executing his trademark flying dismount.

Then he donned the famous St Leger jockey winner's cap, a garment that marked his tenth British Classic triumph. Dettori had earned his prize. And so had Scorpion.

The Irish raider had long been hot favourite for the 229th running of the world's oldest Classic.

Second to Hurricane Run in the Irish Derby, he had gone to Longchamp and demolished Group 1 opposition in the Grand Prix de Paris. Then, the ground had been fast.

Yesterday it was desperately heavy, but it did not stop him winning.

Edgy before the start, he set off in front and never saw another rival. Having set only a steady early gallop, he piled on the pressure up the straight, repelling rivals one by one, only to nearly jettison his finest hour by veering suddenly into the rail after Dettori gave him a proper smack just inside the final furlong.

But this Leger was never going to be lost and, although The Geezer fought valiantly in his attempt to bridge the gap, it was a gap that was never going to be bridged.

'I felt that if somebody came at me I'd pull out a bit more,' added Dettori. 'When I asked him for a final effort he went to quicken again and lost his footing – he was trying to please me so much. He will be a better horse on better ground.'

Whatever Scorpion was to do in the future – and he won the 2007 Coronation Cup under Mick Kinane – the one certainty was that L. Dettori

With the St Leger cap, traditionally presented to the winning jockey of the world's oldest Classic.

would not be involved. He had won another St Leger, but had jeopardized a job, as Paul Eacott reported.

Frankie Dettori yesterday revealed that he would never again ride for Aidan O'Brien, after his decision to partner Scorpion in the St Leger had left 'a sour taste' with Sheikh Mohammed and the Godolphin team.

In a forthright interview on Radio Five Live, the former champion jockey wrote off his injury-hit season as 'crap' and put Dubawi's controversial defeat in the Queen Elizabeth II Stakes, when he ignored the orders given to him by the Godolphin hierarchy, down to the fact that he got 'confused'.

Speaking on the Simon Mayo show, Dettori described his decision to ride Scorpion for Godolphin's chief rivals Coolmore as a 'mistake'.

Asked whether he would ride for O'Brien again, he answered with a simple 'no'. 'The ride was going spare and my team didn't have any horses in the race, so for once I offered my services to the other side,' said Dettori.

'Basically, I just did my job by winning another race, but in hindsight it perhaps wasn't the best thing to do.

'It's like Michael Schumacher one day driving for Ferrari and then driving another car. I didn't do anything wrong, as it was an important race and I thought the horse could win, so I rode it and I did my job. But it left a bit of a sour taste with everybody, so perhaps I shouldn't have done it.

'They are our main rivals and you can't be black one day and then white another day. I made a winning mistake, but it doesn't reflect well on my team when they see me ride for the main opposition. But you learn by your mistakes.'

The three-time champion's hopes of retaining his title came to an end when he broke a collarbone at Sandown in July, but he put his total of just 87 winners for the season down to a combination of factors.

'It was crap, really,' said Dettori. 'I had probably one of my worst seasons. I had a bad injury when I broke my collarbone and I was out for two months.

'The horses did not perform like they can and I did not perhaps ride as well as I can.

'But I had a great season last year and it goes like that – maybe I'll have a good time next year.

'The hardest thing is when you see your own horses winning, as you should have been there – that's what really hurts. First of all financially and then being part of the success. You want to be there yourself, you don't want somebody else taking your success.'

Much of the blame for Dubawi's defeat at the hands of Starcraft in the QEII was put on Dettori's decision to ignore instructions and follow Rakti into the middle of the track. He again confessed yesterday that he had been at fault for the three-quarter-length defeat.

'I was told to go left and then I went right –I just got confused. It was my fault. My boss gives me free rein to do what I think is best at the time and that is why I took that decision.

'It was completely different to what I expected, so I thought I was going to do something which I believed was best. What happened, I didn't expect, and I took the wrong choice. I had to hold my hands up when I made the mistake, but my boss did forgive me.'

Twelve years earlier there had been a much more open breach with his early mentor Luca Cumani. But that had now been long forgiven, and at the end of November, Luca was very pleased that this should be so – as he told Nicholas Godfrey.

Luca Cumani hailed Frankie Dettori as the 'best rider we've seen for a very long time' after teaming up with his favourite former pupil to record a heart-stopping victory in yesterday's Japan Cup with rags-to-riches horse Alkaased, who broke the track record at Tokyo racecourse.

In a nail-biting finale in front of a 95,635 crowd the five-year-old – bought as a handicapper for 42,000gns two years ago by Monaco-based owner Mike Charlton – crossed the line seemingly in unison with domestic hope Heart's Cry.

It was an agonising few minutes before Alkaased's number appeared on the screens to confirm that he had become the first British-trained winner of the £2.5million event since Pilsudski in 1997 – by a nose.

Even then there was a stewards' enquiry before it was confirmed that Dettori had added to his victories on Singspiel (1996) and Falbrav (2002).

Back in third was Zenno Rob Roy, the Japanese superstar bidding to become the first horse to win back-to-back Japan Cups.

Of the other visitors, Ouija Board finished a close-up fifth after making her play early in the straight in a race run on bone-hard ground.

Bago finished eighth after being struck into and losing a shoe, while Warrsan was thirteenth.

Dettori appeared more emotional than usual after winning such a lucrative contest for his mentor Cumani, to whom he was apprenticed.

As soon as the result was announced, Dettori embraced Cumani, to huge cheers from the enormous grandstand.

'I cannot believe it,' said Dettori. 'It means a huge amount to me to win this race for Luca. It's like a dream to be able to win the Japan Cup for the third time. Japan, arigato [thank you]!' Dettori's affection for his old boss was reciprocated, although Cumani could not resist a joke.

'Obviously I hate the little bastard!' he said.

'When he came to England he was basically a pest and he still is a pest. But he is probably the best rider we've seen in the world for a very, very long time.'

On being praised by a local journalist for his skills in bringing Alkaased back from injury to win this contest, Cumani said: 'I think more than being skilled, I'm lucky. Probably not running in the Breeders' Cup made him a bit fresher.'

As for tactics, Cumani claimed to have allowed his rider a free hand. 'I left the strategy to Frankie,' he said. 'As usual, Frankie did it in perfect style.'

'Is someone recording this?' joked the rider, who suggested that Cumani's instructions had been somewhat more specific.

'We were drawn 14 – Luca said, 'you must get over to the rail'.' I said: 'Who do you think I am, Houdini?'

Who exactly someone is can often be encapsulated in their choice of records on Desert Island Discs, *the long-standing BBC Radio 4 programme in which 'castaways' reveal themselves through their choice of eight favourite records. Whether that was so in Dettori's case when he was Sue Lawley's castaway on the programme in January 2006, the extent to which the Derby remained 'unfinished business' was unmistakable. David Carr had his ear to the radio.*

Shame the Scottish Derby has been scrapped. Frankie Dettori could have been just the man to entertain the big-race crowd at Ayr after he revealed an unexpected musical ambition yesterday.

The champion jockey chose 'Amazing Grace' as one of his eight *Desert Island Discs* and told interviewer Sue Lawley that the song, which Ronnie Wood played at his wedding, makes him cry every time he hears it. He also said: 'I am not a musician whatsoever, but if I had to learn one instrument it would be the bagpipes, to be able to play 'Amazing Grace'.

'Wouldn't it be some party trick? "Honey, get the bagpipes out - we've got some friends round!"'

Dettori also revealed he was a punter before his riding days, and collected nearly £2,000 when West Tip won the Grand National in 1986 – thanks to a tip from winning jockey Richard Dunwoody's father George.

'He said to me, "My son's going to win the National this year" and I believed him,' Dettori recalled. 'So I used to go every weekend to place my £5 on it.

'I think I won short of £2,000 and I was only about fifteen. I bought a moped and I bought my landlady a washing machine.'

Dettori shouldn't have been gambling as he was under the legal age at the time, but he said: 'It was easy for me to get into betting shops because in Newmarket everybody is the same size – we are all five foot.'

Dettori, who nominated Dubai Millennium as the best horse he has ridden, also told BBC Radio 4 listeners that he doesn't see himself emulating Lester Piggott by riding into his fifties.

Asked how long he planned to stay in the saddle, he said: 'I am 35 and I would say because I love the job so much, as long as I stay healthy, I think another ten years.

'Lester Piggott is Lester Piggott and you can't compare him to anyone else. I want to do something else.'

The self-confessed wine-lover picked a 'lifetime supply of Pinot Grigio' as his luxury object to take on to his island, but his choice of book was designed to help break his duck in the Derby.

'It is the one thing missing from my CV. I've won everything else in the world and it would be nice to say, "I've done everything", but right now I haven't,' said Dettori.

'The book I have to take is The History of the Derby Stakes, because I have never won it – maybe that will give me a few tips how to win it!'

The year 2006 set off well enough when Electrocutionist won the Dubai World Cup for Godolphin and Dettori to give the jockey his third and the stable their fourth win in the race. But soon after the horses running in the blue silks came to England their form went so awry that they had to temporarily suspend operations. By the time they got their mojo back, it already seemed too late.

David Lawrence caught up with Frankie early in June.

Frankie Dettori has dismissed his chances of regaining the jockeys' championship, despite the 779-1 five-timer at Goodwood on Saturday that encouraged bookmakers to shorten his odds to as low as 12-1.

Dettori's quintet of victories at the Sussex venue – which Coral spokesman Simon Clare estimated cost the industry £2 million – took his total for the season to 37, but the three-time former champion admitted yesterday that recapturing the crown is 'not a priority', although William Hill trimmed him to 12-1 (from 16) yesterday.

He said: 'It was brilliant to ride five winners at Goodwood, especially on a Saturday, when so many people who back my mounts will have had their 50p bets on, but I'm not getting carried away enough by it to think I can win the title again.

'I'm still about thirty behind Jamie Spencer, who's had a good head-start on me, and I certainly won't be chasing around to banded meetings trying to make up the lost ground.

'If I do have a successful run – and the two recent winners from Godolphin suggest the stable that gives me most of my victories is beginning to fire at the rate we usually expect – then I've got a chance of climbing up the table.

'But there's a long way to go before I can be seriously thought of as a possible championship contender and, as I've won it three times before, it's not a priority.'

Dettori added: 'My main aim is to be in the best possible shape for the big races – that's what Godolphin pay me for – and that means avoiding burn-out by racing around the country for two or three mundane meetings per day.

'The fixture list has changed a lot over the past couple of years, since the racecourses were given the opportunity to compete for

A round of golf in Dubai, 2006.

OVERLEAF: Frankie's third Dubai World Cup – on Electrocutionist in 2006.

151

Another angle on a sensational victory … and opposite, horse and jockey return in glory.

meetings, and the travelling involved in riding at two tracks in one day can get to you if you're not careful.

'If I did have a good run and found myself in with a shout of winning the championship in the autumn, then you can be sure I'd give it my best shot, but I'm definitely not putting it at the top of my list of targets, so quoting prices about me to win it is unrealistic.'

Dettori was considerably more optimistic about the way in which, after a slow start to the campaign, Godolphin has signalled a revival in its fortunes with the victories of Librettist at Nottingham last week and Satchem in Saturday's On The House Stakes at Goodwood. He said: 'Those two wins were very encouraging and I'm hoping now that the stable can get into top gear.

'Satchem showed a lot of guts to fight back after being headed at Goodwood, and horses who do that have to be fit and in form, so I hope it's a good sign for the whole team.

'Simon [Crisford] and Saeed [bin Suroor] have been telling everyone we're two weeks behind and that's right – but, given a clear run now, I'm hoping we can start to make that up.

'There are important meetings not too far away, including Royal Ascot, of course, and they're the places I need to be making sure I'm at my best.

'I don't want people to start thinking Frankie Dettori has made a comeback just because he's ridden five winners in a day, even though that's very hard to do. I want them to think he's never been away.'

Despite their jockey's belated optimism, 2006 was to prove a miserable year for Godolphin. They did not have a single Group 1 winner in England and of the three in France, the first did not come until Librettist slogged through heavy ground to win the Prix Jacques le Marois at Deauville. For Dettori, tellingly, the big horses would have to come from other stables, and on them he could still show that there was nothing wrong with his skill set, given the right machinery underneath it.

Never more so that season than at Goodwood, where he was the leading jockey. His winners there included Sixties Icon, on whom he would win the St Leger a month later, and Ouija Board, whose sustained duel with Alexander Goldrun in the Nassau Stakes went down into legend. Frankie and Ouija Board would share another great day when winning at the Breeders' Cup in New York, where the rider was also successful with Red Rocks. But it was the Peter Chapple-Hyam colt Authorized, on whom he had won the Racing Post Trophy at Newbury, that was the name to treasure in the winter – because he just might be the one to put that Derby omission right.

Come 2007, first impressions were good, and Tony Elves reported from Newmarket's Craven meeting that Frankie had been excited after a gallop on Authorized before racing.

The expected decision that Authorized would go for the Totesport Dante Stakes rather than the Stan James Two Thousand Guineas was confirmed after the Peter Chapple-Hyam-trained colt worked over seven and a half furlongs.

Authorized had been displaying staying tendencies in his recent work on the Limekilns trial ground, and he lengthened to go a couple of lengths clear of an older lead horse yesterday. The gallop was watched by the colt's co-owner Saleh Al Homaizi.

Chapple-Hyam said: 'Authorized will go for the Dante and won't run in the Two Thousand Guineas. We brought him here to wake him up and it has gone well. Frankie Dettori was very happy with him, but he's a typical Montjeu and is so laid back – he does everything so easy.'

Dettori was delighted with the effort of Authorized, who sprung a 25-1 surprise for him in the Racing Post Trophy, although in terms of

Vodafone Derby rides he could be obliged to partner Eastern Anthem if the Godolphin number one hope makes it to Epsom.

'That was good,' said Dettori of the gallop. 'He has done very well physically and I am glad he was brought here as he needed this to wake him up. This will really bring him forward and he will come out of this bouncing.'

Authorized duly won the Dante well enough to make him a short-priced favourite to lay Frankie's Epsom hoodoo.

But the fates were not going to let us get there without a scare. Tony Elves again:

Frankie Dettori yesterday dispelled doubts over his fitness by riding red-hot Vodafone Derby favourite Authorized in a workout on the Newmarket gallops.

Dettori, who damaged a knee ligament in a mid-race fall at Goodwood on Friday, said he intends to return to the saddle tomorrow evening at Sandown – and also gave a firm hint that he is planning to ride for at least another ten years.

Frankie on the great Ouija Board: at home in Newmarket (above), and (opposite) in furious Goodwood action against Kevin Manning on Alexander Goldrun in the famous Nassau Stakes finish of 2006.

Dettori, 36, has been receiving medical treatment since his mishap on Fort Amhurst at the Sussex track, but he proved he is on the mend by partnering the Peter Chapple-Hyam-trained Authorized over a mile on the Limekilns.

He said: 'On Saturday morning, I couldn't really walk. I had physio, ultrasound treatment and acupuncture. The knee improved throughout the day and I had more physio with ultrasound on Saturday night.

'I was very keen to see Authorized work this morning at eight o'clock. But by that stage I felt really eager to sit on him myself.

'I still had pain but didn't feel as uncomfortable as Saturday.'

Giving an insight into what life has been like in the past week, Dettori said: 'It doesn't matter which shop or taxi I go in, everyone is wishing me the best of luck. I don't think I've ever been in such a media spotlight before – not for a race. I guess the horse has captured a lot of people's minds.'

Authorized out on his own in the Dante Stakes at York, May 2007.

Frankie was not exaggerating about the media spotlight, as Alastair Down exemplified.

There is only one certainty about Saturday's Derby – it won't be won by Authorized. The favourite may well hose up like a good thing as Epsom erupts about his ears, but for once the horse will not be the hour's hero. It'll be 'Frankie wot won it', just as it was 54 years ago when that popular pixie of public esteem and affection, Sir Gordon Richards, finally slew his Derby dragon on Pinza, sparking national rejoicing.

So if you don't like your sporting heroes to be good-looking Italians who weigh in at around eight and a half stone and can milk an audience better than any theatrical knight, then now is the time to ring Ryanair or Eurostar, because somewhere abroad is the place for you to be.

They say 'uneasy lies the head that wears a crown', but you can bet Lombard Street to a china orange that during the run-up to the Derby it hasn't lain half as uneasy as the head in the Dettori household that is desperate to put it on.

To be fair, Dettori has already run a big race this week. Like no other jockey, he understands that he has a role to play for racing, and although he may be climbing the walls mentally as the Derby looms, he knows he has to ride the media merry-go-round. Last Sunday, he hosted a press conference at Newmarket and was at his most animated and affable, more quotable than Oscar Wilde and with the charm throttle open wide.

Then I managed to mug him at home, as the BBC and Clare Balding set up for interviews ahead of a potentially enormous day's TV for racing, which presents that rare opportunity of bringing a mass audience what it most wants to see.

Of course, this level of intrusion must sometimes be a rectal pain, but he understands it is part of the territory and says: 'It's an entertainment sport – racing is for the public. If there is a big crowd on an important day they want me to jump off, and if you don't do it then you get booed because it's a little part of what they are there for. I learned long ago that if you go along with it all you make it much easier for yourself.

'There is a part of me that is trying not to think about the race but it is impossible, as it is all anyone, including your friends, wants to

PREVIOUS SPREAD: An eagle's eye
view of Authorized romping home in
the 2007 Derby.

talk about. But it is the hardest thing to win – I've had fourteen rides
in it and almost always I have been dead five furlongs out.

'First, the two of us have to get to the race in one piece, and then
all I want is a clean shot at it – then it is up to me whether I screw it
up or not. That's why I am so nervous about it.

'Every Derby is about unknown territory. Apart from the human
side you ask, "Will he stay, will he not stay?" and "Will he act, will he
not act?"

'And it is full of horses who are still unknown quantities. In the
King George, if you are on a 20-1 shot it is just that – a 20-1 shot. But
in the Derby you can still win on a 20-1 shot and that is what makes it
unique.'

The Dettori home, just outside Newmarket, is pleasant enough
from the outside and like the Tardis once you are through the door,
a vast split-level open-plan kitchen/sitting room with a TV nicked
from a multiplex, a bar and loads of kids' paraphernalia – and why
not, as this is the house of a man who happily admits: 'I never really
matured!'

You wonder where he would be without wife Catherine who, to
continue the Doctor Who analogy, is the type of smart, sexy and
resourceful woman who makes a fabulous assistant to the great man.
Catherine and the children are in Disneyland Paris for the weekend
and Frankie says: 'Doesn't the place seem empty without them all?'

There must have been a long period when there wasn't much
worth watching on the big TV, as Catherine and Frankie have five
children, from just under eight years old down to two and a half. The
walls show off wonderful enlarged black and white shots of the tribe
and, let's face it, it is in the Italian genes to get out of your jeans and
make hundreds of babies.

Those who knew Frankie when he first arrived in Britain with
£366 in his pocket from his father will vouch that he was a busy
bunny on this front. With a huge beam, but no trace of smugness or
smirking, he announces: 'Hey, I was unstoppable in those days.'

He would certainly have taken some mentoring. His father,
Gianfranco, was tough on his son in the manner of many successful

fathers, and the guiding hands on the tiller were principally provided by the formidable half-back line of Luca Cumani, John Gosden and Barney Curley in the Norman Hunter role.

Nor, I suspect, is Frankie the type of man to forget his benefactors and those who saw qualities in him as human and horseman that were worth nurturing. Yes, his achievements are his own, but your real friends in life transform their weight from that of flesh to gold when things are rough, and he has never been short of folk to sit up late with him when the mood was dark.

Even if the child in Frankie is alive and well, there has never been anything infantile about him in the saddle, and on his day he remains something exceptional to watch. But if it wasn't for the jockeyship there would be none of the showmanship, and the riches, restaurants and star status don't rest on a winning smile but on the necessary passion to win.

He is very much a Godolphin man these days. There have been times when he has had to be gently reminded that he is a jockey first and foremost and a personality second, but Sheikh Mohammed has always had a soft spot for his jockey and indulged him like a favourite son. There is a rumour that Sheikh Hamdan is occasionally heard mischievously to mutter, 'What about Swain … ?' half under his breath, but there has never been an ego that didn't benefit from the occasional tug on the choke chain.

After Authorized won the Dante, Frankie played it by the book, saying he would ride whatever Godolphin chose to run in the Derby. Sheikh Mohammed doesn't sit around doing nothing all day – there is a country to run, state visits to fulfil and an economy expanding like a supernova – but the decision came the next day and Frankie was immediately released. No shilly-shallying, no power games, no playing with people's lives, and as Frankie says: 'What's more, he wants me to win it.'

And so do so many of the rest of us. There will be the usual moaning minnies who insist that it is all about the horse – but Saturday simply isn't about the horse, it is about the man with a washing machine turning over at full cycle in his stomach.

Opening Frankie's Bar and Grill with Marco Pierre White, 2006.

It is only a partial exaggeration to say that in two days' time Dettori's career distils into two minutes. Imagine Tiger Woods without a Masters win or John McEnroe never successful at Wimbledon. It wouldn't make them lesser players, but the failure on the day that mattered most would detract from the otherwise triumphant whole, those final feet to the top of Everest remaining elusive and unconquered.

And don't doubt that he will die a thousand deaths as the time to mount the scaffold approaches, and we find out whether it is for a coronation or an execution. He may be a tough three-time champion with 2,500 winners under his belt, but inevitably this one winner has the capacity to dwarf them all.

The public have come to love this bouncy Italian with his accent from central casting. He will ride a magic carpet of goodwill, but there is also half a ton of racehorse to thread round the trickiest track on the planet under more pressure than a submarine in the deepest ocean trench. He has brought a mighty amount to this sport and, while he has taken plenty back, he would swap most of it and his right arm for this Derby. Dettori is more than good enough to play his part. Let's hope the bloody horse is.

For once the horse had read the script, and Jon Lees filed the Racing Post's *main report on a very special race.*

Authorised by Sheikh Mohammed, authorised by destiny. Frankie Dettori jubilantly fulfilled his dream yesterday.

After fourteen failures at Epsom he got what he had always wished for, as a coveted first Derby triumph slipped into the grasp of the man formerly known as the greatest jockey never to taste victory in racing's greatest Classic.

Successful in every other British Classic at least twice, winner of many of the world's greatest races, and author of his own Magnificent Seven, when he rode every winner on the card at Ascot in 1996, Dettori had done virtually everything else there was to do in the sport.

This storyline had been prepared for many years, but it required a horse with the brilliance of the Peter Chapple-Hyam-trained Authorized to ensure that Dettori saw it through to the right conclusion.

Yes, the pressure was on, but no-one was to be let down, such was the superiority Authorized, the 5-4 favourite, held over his rivals in the Vodafone Derby yesterday as he raced to a win that inflicted what bookmakers claimed was 'the heaviest defeat ever in the Derby'.

There was an extra spring in the legs of the delirious Italian as he performed his famous flying dismount from the back of Authorized into the arms of his tearful father, Gianfranco.

'This is a dream come true,' he said.

'I've been waiting so long to do this. I haven't slept for two weeks, but this was the first day I've felt all right. Now all the bullshit was out of the way, I just had to keep focused and do my job.

'It was a long two and a half minutes and they went a serious gallop. I counted the horses in front of me coming down the hill and I think there were ten, but I knew if they kept up the gallop there wouldn't be a problem.

'At the four-and-a-half pole, I had a peep under my arm and I could only see daylight. I got him balanced going to the two-furlong marker and he stretched away.

'When I got past the furlong marker the world stopped, my heart stopped, I knew this was going to be my moment. Everything went so smoothly. I expected a dog fight but it was like an oil painting, beautiful and smooth.'

Authorized started slowly and was further back in the field than was ideal, but Dettori stayed out of danger and set out to track Strategic Prince down the hill to Tattenham Corner.

Once into the straight, only one result appeared likely, and when Dettori produced the colt to make his challenge, Authorized, tongue lolling out, quickly pulled well clear of the field, coming home five lengths in front of Eagle Mountain, with Aqaleem beating Lucarno in the photo-finish for third.

'After we crossed the line, nobody could get to me,' Dettori said. 'I could hear people saying well done, but they were a furlong behind. I wanted to cry, be happy. I haven't had a chance to sit down and have a proper cry.'

Chapple-Hyam had experienced Derby success before, but memories of his triumph fifteen years ago with Dr Devious were 'a haze'. This was an occasion he was determined to enjoy.

'I don't take drugs, but I smoke and drink - this is better than anything,' he said. 'Authorized was probably further back than he wanted to be, but he got the perfect ride in the perfect race from the perfect horse.'

Part-owner Imad Sagar said: 'When I heard Frankie was free to ride today, it was great news. I even planned to have a talk with Sheikh Mohammed, or even visit him.'

Dettori said: 'I can't state enough how great Sheikh Mohammed has been to me. I've worked for him for thirteen years and he's the guy who pays the bills. If it wasn't for him, I would not have been in the position to win today, and if I win the Derby again one day I hope it will be for him.

'One day, when I retire, I can safely say I have conquered my sport. I have achieved everything I want to achieve. It's nice to say I've done it.'

When Frankie is surfing the wave of success something very special runs down the reins. In little more than a fortnight after Epsom he had won the French Derby on Lawman, the Gran Premio Milano on Sudan and, most crucially of all, had given Godolphin their first Group 1 success in Britain for three years when getting Ramonti home in a four-way photo-finish for the Queen Anne Stakes at Royal Ascot.

The roll continued into Goodwood. Earlier in the year Frankie had lived what he called 'every schoolboy's dream' when being taken round the motor racing track by Formula One champion Fernando Alonso. But with the horses it was time for him and his employers to show that they too have worn the crown. Jon Lees again:

The Goodwood revival celebrates a golden era in motor sport, but there was an air of nostalgia on another part of the estate yesterday,

With his first Derby in the bag, Frankie goes to Chantilly the following day and wins the Prix du Jockey Club.

when Godolphin enjoyed their best day on the track in Britain for three years.

At its peak as dominant as Ferrari, such occasions for Sheikh Mohammed's elite team were becoming a distant memory until Ramonti and two-year-old Rio De La Plata put the stable back on the podium yesterday.

At Royal Ascot, Ramonti recorded Godolphin's first British victory at Group 1 level since August 2005 – Punctilious in the Yorkshire Oaks – and he added the second in the BGC Sussex Stakes, the highlight of day two of the meeting.

The theme for the afternoon had already been set by the exciting Rio De La Plata, whose victory in the Group 2 Veuve Clicquot Vintage Stakes teed up trainer Saeed bin Suroor for his first Pattern-race double in Britain since the 2004 Royal Meeting, when Papineau and Punctilious won the Gold Cup and Ribblesdale Stakes.

The underperformance of the stable has been the focus of much comment in the media. However, that appeared of no consequence to the sheikh, who delivered an enthusiastic vote of confidence in his team.

He said: 'This is a free country and you can write what you want, but I have different ideas. I have a great team. I think they're the best in the world, and I'm very happy.'

His racing manager Simon Crisford took up the thread. 'Nothing has changed since three years ago, when Saeed bin Suroor was champion trainer and we won £4 million in prize-money. The only thing that's changed is the horses, and we have different horses now to then.

'Last season and this season were disappointing by our standards, but you can play only with the cards in your hand, and that's what we've been doing.

Sheikh Mohammed (right) and Saeed bin Suroor with Frankie and Ramonti after the Queen Anne Stakes, 2007.

'What goes around comes around, and hopefully we'll have some good horses in the future.'

Ramonti, forced over the line by Frankie Dettori at Ascot, required far less coercion from the jockey yesterday, when the race was set up perfectly for him by the Ballydoyle pair Archipenko and Trinity College, who led the field.

Produced to lead two furlongs out, the ex-Italian five-year-old was in front soon enough but stuck on gamely, although he had only a head to spare at the line over the closing Excellent Art, with Jeremy third.

Ramonti is the first horse to win the Queen Anne and Sussex Stakes in the same season since Rousillon in 1985.

Bin Suroor, saddling his third winner at the meeting, looked forward to better times. He said: 'It was a very tough race to win, but our horses are flying at this time. I would be happy to see him run in the Queen Elizabeth II Stakes. The horse is improving all the time.

'This is a happy day. The season started quietly, but from December I knew what quality of horses we had. I'm not really that surprised by the way they have run.

'Early in the season you have to run the three-year-olds. Some of them have never run in Group 1s, but you have to give them a chance to do well. The three-year-olds we have aren't really good enough, and only Measured Tempo has won a Listed race.

'This year, I think the two-year-olds are much better than we had last year or the year before. There is always the pressure there and you have to be really patient.

'You cannot win everything, and you can't lose everything, but must keep looking to the future.'

For the jockey, his main stable was back in shape, but his more immediate task was to see if he could get Authorized back to winning ways after being outmanoeuvred in the Eclipse at Sandown. It was a task which he approached with confidence but not good health. Jon Lees was on the Knavesmire.

There is still no cure for the common cold, but Frankie Dettori could vouch for the medicinal qualities of a Juddmonte International triumph on Authorized, which gave both the virus-stricken jockey and the bruised reputation of the Derby winner a timely pick-me-up yesterday.

Despite recording a five-length victory in the Epsom Classic, Authorized's subsequent defeat in the Coral-Eclipse Stakes by Notnowcato had put the Peter Chapple-Hyam-trained colt's credibility back under the microscope.

Yet after the rematch, in which Authorized and Notnowcato were joined by the King George winner Dylan Thomas, the evidence was much clearer.

At the end of a contest this time not determined by tactical enterprise, Authorized crossed the line a length clear of Dylan Thomas, with last year's winner Notnowcato three lengths further back in third, to become the first Derby winner since 2002 hero High Chaparral to win a subsequent race.

Chapple-Hyam said: 'I'm delighted for everyone, mainly the horse. This probably means more than the Derby because he got beat and everyone was knocking him. I have to read it every day, but luckily he can't read. It doesn't bother me, but I worry about the horse.

'There has been a lot of pressure to make him win. I wanted him to show he was as good a horse as I said he was, but I knew if I did everything right it would be all over.'

That was very much Dettori's experience too, as Authorized travelled with ease until approaching the furlong pole, from where he put the race to bed when forging into a clear lead that Dylan Thomas proved unable to overcome.

'In the Eclipse, everyone went out there to try to outfox me,' said Dettori. 'I was watching George Washington and Notnowcato was the one who got away. Today there was nowhere to hide and Authorized put the record straight. He is now up there as one of the best horses I've ridden. I'm delighted he's proved to the world what we thought he was.

'I've been sick as a dog for the last two weeks and I refused to take antibiotics because I didn't want to feel bad, but this is the best tonic riding him today.

'Between the three pole and the one and a half, the further he was going the harder it was to hold him. He was pulling a cart and when I saw Dylan Thomas angling out, I got three lengths and the race was over.

'Once he's in front, he just does what he has to do. He has tremendous cruising speed and that's what separates him from being a normal champion. I can't wait for the Arc.'

For Authorized the Arc was definitely not worth waiting for – he ran no race at all and finished third from last. So while there was still a Group 1 to come when Rio De La Plata won the Prix Jean-Luc Lagadere on Arc day, the enduring star for Dettori and for Godolphin was Ramonti. Two great days were up ahead. The first at Ascot in September, witnessed by Jon Lees.

Rio De La Plata wins the Prix Jean-Luc Lagardere, October 2007.

OPPOSITE: Washing down at the Breeders' Cup, 2007.

From the multitude of available talent, only one horse has kept delivering the goods at the top level this year for Godolphin, who yesterday gave thanks to the qualities of the redoubtable Ramonti.

The stable's Group 1 triumphs in Europe this year have all been his, and the ex-Italian proved himself one of the toughest to race for the team's cause with his third top-flight win of the season.

Despite winning the Queen Anne and Sussex Stakes, Ramonti hasn't gained the profile of former Saeed bin Suroor-trained stars, but his claim to top the mile rankings were considerably strengthened by a battling win in the Queen Elizabeth II Stakes under Frankie Dettori.

Ramonti had a score to settle with the filly Darjina, who beat him in the Prix du Moulin, and a point to prove to Excellent Art, the Ballydoyle colt some considered an unlucky loser in the Sussex Stakes.

He managed both in typically determined style, Dettori throwing down a challenge to his rivals over two furlongs out that they were unable to match.

When international handicappers meet to determine the mile pecking order, they will consider the merits of Manduro, who won the Prix Jacques le Marois, but in the winner's enclosure Dettori was telling Ramonti: 'You're the champion now.'

Addressing a wider audience, he added: 'He beat George Washington twice and now we've beaten all the others again and he proved he truly deserves to be champion miler. He's won the three major miles races of Britain and has been ultra-consistent.

'I've been nervous all day because I knew Ramonti had a great chance. I was a little concerned about the ground but I made sure it was a good mile, and from two and a half out I said, "Come and get me." I knew they had to have the legs to get to me and pass me, and that's very hard to do with Ramonti. He's a proper fighter.

'He has become a revelation. I rode him in the Lockinge and didn't ride him with too much confidence and waited too long, but as I got to know him better I've learned I have to take the fight to them. Without a doubt, he is one of the toughest horses I have ridden.'

Ramonti was not done with yet and in December went to Hong Kong for his seasonal swansong. Dettori got there via an unsuccessful Breeders' Cup and a last-gasp success in the exotic racing outpost that is Mauritius. It had been an eventful year in every sense and this was the best of ways to end it. Paul Eacott joined the crush at Sha Tin.

Don't you just love it when a plan comes together? Judging by the smiles, Godolphin certainly do. And boy, what a plan.

Having confirmed himself as the best miler in Europe with wins in the Queen Anne, Queen Elizabeth II and Sussex Stakes during the summer, there looked an obvious target for Ramonti to round off his season in Hong Kong. Bypassing the Breeders' Cup in favour of a trip to the Far East, another crack at the milers looked the way to go.

However, the five-year-old's connections decided to overlook the obvious and instead gamble on Ramonti staying the extra two furlongs of the Cup, the principal event of yesterday's Cathay Pacific-sponsored four-race series at Sha Tin. In the end it was a gamble well worth taking.

Settled in third behind early pacesetter Royal Prince and Japan's Shadow Gate, Ramonti glided down the Sha Tin back straight hard on the steel, and when Frankie Dettori decided to let him go, it was clear that one horse was a cut above the others.

Ramonti and Frankie after winning the Hong Kong Cup, 2007.

The only doubt about the outcome emerged after Dettori and Ramonti had come home half a length clear of Viva Pataca and Mick Kinane, as winning connections had to wait on the outcome of a stewards' enquiry and an objection by Kinane before they were able to lift the weighty-looking Hong Kong Cup.

Saeed bin Suroor, who became the first trainer to achieve two Cup wins, now reckons this 1m2f trip suits Ramonti better than 1m.

'This is the best distance for him,' he said. 'He won three Group 1s and was the champion miler in Europe, but he always looked like he needed further.

'Frankie gave him a brilliant ride to make sure he finished his race, and we know now which way we will be going with him.'

Dettori, who also won the Cup on Godolphin's Fantastic Light in 2000 and the Luca Cumani-trained Falbrav in 2003, added: 'He's one of the bravest I have ridden – he really tries for you. He was a bit keen early on with the slow pace, but I knew it would take a real good one to get by me. He is one of the best.'

For Frankie that Derby hoodoo had been laid and Godolphin were back on track. But strains were showing in the relationship. Seeds of doubt had been sown. It would take a while, but in time there would be a bitter harvest.

THE SLIPPERY SLOPE

PREVIOUS SPREAD: Penny for his
thoughts ...

W hat do you do when you have done everything ? If you are Frankie Dettori you just try to do it all over again, and any dip in success starts up the rumour mill.

After Authorized had finally laid the Dettori Derby hoodoo at Epsom in 2007 there were always going to be moments for others – and maybe even for Frankie – to wonder about his motivation.

For although in 2008 he landed Group 1s for Godolphin, captained the British team in the Shergar Cup, did charity work for the Starlight Foundation, won the St Leger for Sir Michael Stoute on Conduit and delivered his owners winnings of more than £2.2 million in the UK alone, his numbers were down to 67 from that resurgent 2004 total of 195, and Godolphin's £4 million score for 2004 was down to a 'mere' £2 million plus in 2008.

So as the year moved on to its overseas climax at the Breeders' Cup at Santa Anita, Frankie felt he had a position to defend as he and the Racing Post's James Willoughby chewed the fat.

For two years after the plane crash of 2000, Frankie Dettori lost a sense of purpose. Now time has passed, Dettori seems to inhabit his persona more completely than ever before. In conversation, he does not head off difficult questions and is far less prone to glib rejoinders than others.

Moreover, he engages with tricky subjects fluently, philosophically and seemingly with ease.

By his own admission, Dettori will always be an excitable, mercurial character, a livewire who presents an easily definable image to his public. But he appears a little more reflective than before.

When the subject of criticism arose, he started as many do. 'Whatever people say about me, I don't care nowadays. I gave all that up on 1 June 2000. I will live my life the way I want to do. I love it.

'I feel like my performance is much better when I am happy within myself. When you live in the spotlight, it is inevitable you will attract negative comments from time to time. People say you're good, people say you're bad. What does it matter really?'

Of course, we all know it matters.

In Dubai.

The need to be respected, loved, whatever, is human nature. Nobody is invulnerable. And anyone denying it will contradict themselves sooner or later.

Dettori held out for fifteen minutes. 'I will be honest with you,' he said when confronted with the concept that Godolphin are underachieving. 'I feel there is a lot of negativity towards us for some reason. I feel a bit hurt about it. From maidens to Group 1s, we try very hard 100 per cent of the time.

'I am the one at the forefront of my stable, in the battlefield, so I am the one who hears it and who sees it.

'Look, it is the same team as fourteen years ago. We have had some fantastic times, raced some great horses, provided some of the great moments in the sport's history.

'We haven't had a good time this year, I accept it, but I don't think the level of criticism and the way it is done is appropriate.

'Sheikh Mohammed is 100 per cent behind us and we are doing all the same things we used to do. I understand that people have a right to comment, but it goes too far, too much.

Getting the hump. Frankie visits the desert outside Dubai in 2008.

'You ask me why? No idea … I think jealousy.'

Interestingly, Dettori seems more perturbed by criticism of Godolphin than of himself. On the latter, it is fair to say that his words and actions have not always been projected as fairly as he deserves.

The best example came in the aftermath of the 2006 Queen Elizabeth II Stakes won by George Washington. The winning trainer Aidan O'Brien described Dettori as 'paranoid' for claiming he had been pushed wide on Librettist by the Ballydoyle pacemaker Ivan Denisovich.

O'Brien also had some other harsh words for Dettori. Did anyone take up Dettori's case? Did anyone say that O'Brien was out of order?

No. Instead, it was recognised that O'Brien was merely defending his position. But not everyone extended the same respect to Dettori.

Listen to his side of it now: 'I said what I had to say. I do not regret that. In the heat of the moment, you have to say things to defend yourself and your team.

'This part of it you can't back down from when people challenge you. I said what I thought was right at the time. It's gone. Aidan and I have shaken hands and moved on, but I am in a competitive business and want to win races.

'It was like when Lewis Hamilton cut the corner and was disqualified after finishing first in the Belgian Grand Prix. Like him, I am going to defend my position, it is all part of the sport. And I respect the right of others to act like myself.'

Doesn't that seem entirely reasonable? Is there a risk that people are too quick to characterise him as fickle, erratic, injudicious on occasions, just because of his extroverted personality?

Those like him who constantly make themselves available become too familiar for their own good, perhaps. Unfairly, their opinion in matters of controversy tends to be regarded as less weighty than those who are more elusive.

But where would we be without Dettori? This man has carried racing on his back for the past fifteen years. He has given it an identity with the younger market of which nobody else has so far been capable.

Sure, he has had his moments, even before the dreadful events of 2000.

But we sometimes forget that the Dettori who presents himself alternately as the clown and the acrobat is also one of the greatest riders to peer through a pair of goggles.

Okay, it's partly his fault if that much is obscured at times. Aside from all the superficial nonsense – the flying dismounts and the branded canned tomatoes – there is so much of genuine fascination about Dettori.

It is understandable if his head has been turned by celebrity, but get him to talk about riding and it soon becomes apparent that there is real substance to his opinions.

His passion for riding knowledge started in the time he spent as a teenager in the US.

'When I was sixteen, just a baby, I did four winters in California,' he said. 'All the greats were there – Pincay, Shoemaker, Stevens, McCarron, Valenzuela. All the gods,' he continued, becoming more animated, widening his eyes perhaps to appear as star-struck as he was back then.

'Phenomenal talents. Unbelievable. As if they weren't enough, Cordero used to fly over for the weekend from New York. Can you imagine what it was like for a young rider like myself?

With Seb Sanders and Hayley Turner – forming the Shergar Cup team, 2008.

Conduit – a fourth St Leger win for Frankie and a first for legendary trainer Sir Michael Stoute, who (opposite) receives the unwelcome attentions of the winning jockey.

'They took me under their wings. Taught me. I was only a baby but among the gods. They gave me great advice. You find your own way in the end, but that was all a great inspiration to me, helped me build a lot of confidence.'

That confidence received a major blow ten years ago to this month. Dettori took the mount on Swain in the Breeders' Cup Classic at Churchill Downs.

A special horse in a special race. A race loaded with talent. Top-class US horses like Skip Away, Touch Gold, Victory Gallop and Gentlemen. It was a chance for Dettori to enter American racing history alongside the names he chronicled above.

Instead, he became part of infamy, whipping the Godolphin warhorse left-handed with such force that he hung right and threw away a winning chance. It was a moment that took a long time to live down.

'Now, when I go to America, I still feel I have something left to prove. Not just for myself but for European jockeys in general.'

The irony of the Swain episode is that Dettori rides dirt races better than any European. He was brilliant on Wilko in the 2004 Breeders' Cup Juvenile, a masterclass in which he put every one of the most important concepts of riding on the surface together. He was even better on Electrocutionist in the 2006 Dubai World Cup.

'Riding on dirt requires a different approach from the grass,' he says. 'You need tactical speed, but you have to use it properly.

'You can't stop and start like you do on the turf. That's the fundamental point. You have to put yourself in a position where you get a clear run, but you mustn't sacrifice ground doing it.

'Polytrack is different again. And every course has its own identity. Wolverhampton, you can't catch them for love nor money, but Lingfield you come from behind easily; if you go too soon, you get caught.

'I like Polytrack for all the reasons that all horsemen do; it is kind on horses' legs. I do think it takes some of the greatness away from horses, though. A bit of immediate speed. A bit of class.

'Nothing can beat the grass. Nothing feels like a great champion stretching out and accelerating underneath you like it feels on grass. It is the natural surface for the horse and you can tell.

'That said, Dubai Millennium in the Dubai World Cup of 2000 is still the greatest moment I have enjoyed in the sport. And that was on dirt. But it was the horse, the way he killed them. It broke my heart when he was retired with an injury. He was only just getting really good. It is hard to believe there will be another, but maybe, just maybe, before I finish, one might come along.'

Dettori has kept himself in the headlines over the past couple of years with a succession of high-profile winners for stables other than Godolphin. But at no time during our meeting did he separate his own success from theirs.

At no time did he excuse his own lack of productivity or reduced strike rate by reference to that of Saeed bin Suroor. He could have done so subtly and without being quoted. He could have asked for any of his comments to remain off the record.

But he didn't because there was never any need. To his mind, the public perception of Dettori and Godolphin are inseparable.

And when Godolphin do return to form, Dettori's mind is right. He is focused, he is happy and he is ready.

Yes, Frankie had come to Hollywood, and for him this Breeders' Cup was a scriptwriter's dream, as Jon Lees reported.

The transformation in Frankie Dettori's Breeders' Cup experience had a touch of Hollywood about it as he went from zero to hero within an extraordinary six hours.

Dettori had taken the rap for the defeat of hot favourite Sixties Icon in the Marathon and seen victory on Diabolical in the Turf Sprint snatched away from him in the last few strides, so his meeting was not going to script.

Yet at the end of judgement day the jockey was taking the congratulations of California governor Arnold 'Terminator' Schwarzenegger after raising his game to carve out one of the most important wins of his career on Raven's Pass in the Classic and crown an extraordinary night of success for British runners.

With Donativum capturing the Juvenile Turf, Dettori, who as a sixteen-year-old came to California to work for John Gosden in 1987, moved alongside Gary Stevens in the number of Breeders' Cup races won. Only four jockeys have secured more than eight victories, of whom only Mike Smith is still riding.

Dettori had a strong book of mounts but, according to trainer Jeremy Noseda, he forgot his lines on his supposed best chance of the

On Raven's Pass after winning the Breeders' Cup Classic at Santa Anita in 2008.

185

'I'll be back.' Frankie and Godolphin's John Ferguson with Arnold Schwarzenegger, Governor of California, after the 2008 Classic.

day, Sixties Icon. His lead on Godolphin's Diabolical lasted until three strides short of the line, but he turned things around on his next mount, Donativum, who collared Westphalia to clinch the Juvenile Turf.

'I love Santa Anita,' he said. 'This is where I started as a young boy. Coming back here to some really great friends has been overwhelming. I knew I had a great book of rides, but when Diabolical got caught on the line, it was very hard to swallow. So I'm doubly excited because of that. Winning a race here, it means so much to me.'

Despite his race record, Dettori has never been allowed to forget his ride on Swain in the 1998 Classic, in which he threw away his chance by whipping the horse across the track. Success on Raven's Pass, on whom he replaced regular rider Jimmy Fortune, lifted that particular monkey off his back.

Gosden said: 'He's had a little bit of a difficult time in the Classic. He wiped out all the cameramen at Churchill Downs on Swain and got touched off a nose by Tiznow on Sakhee in 2001, so you can say the race hasn't entirely gone his way. The monkey was beginning to have his hands around the throat, so he was very pleased to release that.'

Dettori said: 'I've been close twice and I was reminding my wife that perhaps it's a bit of fate that it was ten years ago that I got beat on Swain and that didn't go down very well, and I got close with Sakhee. I had a third chance and didn't want to let it slip.

'I had a good horse, I had a good partner. I'm a little bit older, and I'm not saying wiser, but more experienced. So I was able to tackle the challenge, I was more serene and got the job done.

'Once I got behind Curlin, I said that's half the job done. He's going to take me there, and sure he did. Then it was a worrying moment for a split second when I asked him, would he pick up or would he falter on the distance? But he did pick up.

'The last furlong was a pretty long one, but I could feel that he was still galloping strong and millions of emotions went through my head. When I crossed the line, I didn't really know if it was true or a dream, just that fake reality.

But I realised straight away it was true, and I'm delighted. The Classic for us Europeans is the biggest prestigious race you can ever win. This is personal satisfaction.'

Despite that international boost Frankie and the Godolphin juggernaut continued to attract the doubters, a situation hardly helped at Royal Ascot 2009 when their first eight runners could only log one third placing and their sole success, in the Ribblesdale with Flying Clouds, was with a filly who had been prepared until recently by Andre Fabre in France.

But even if Frankie and Godolphin had to wait until Schiaparelli's Gran Premio del Jockey Club in October to register their first Group 1 of the season, events had turned enough by then for Frankie to have got 100 winners up and the Godolphin score to have lifted to 148 for the UK alone.

By March 2010 Frankie was reaching for the sky again. Howard Wright and Jon Lees jointly filed the story.

Frankie Dettori was set to jet out of Dubai last night for Doncaster today, when he will make an earlier-than-usual start to the Flat turf campaign, having set himself a target of 150 winners this year – a goal he will be helped towards by an initial link-up with Mark Johnston.

Pounced wins the Breeders' Cup Juvenile Turf for Lady Rothschild and John Gosden in November 2009.

Having ridden 100 winners last year for the first time since 2006, Dettori said he wanted the 2010 season to be even more productive, but resisted talk of a challenge for the jockeys' championship, for which he has been a major market mover this week with Skybet to deny titleholder Ryan Moore and chief rival Kieren Fallon.

Last year's back-end rally by Dettori's retaining stable of Godolphin has convinced the jockey, who last topped the championship in 2004 when he rode 192 winners, that 150 is a realistic aim and, as Saeed bin Suroor's string are returning to Newmarket earlier than usual, he is making an immediate start.

'I got to 100 last year, and if my stable finishes the season like it did last year, I should make it to 150,' Dettori said at Meydan yesterday. 'I'm fit, and I want to stay that way, because our horses are coming back from Dubai the week after next, in time to have runners at the Craven meeting. When we didn't come back until the Guineas, there wasn't the same reason for me to start riding early.'

A total of 150 winners would have been enough to win the jockeys' title in 2002 and finish second for four of the last five seasons.

Dettori, who had 103 winners in 2009, after totals of 67 and 77 led some to question his appetite for race-riding, had expected to have three rides at Doncaster, but the softening ground turned against two and his sole engagement is for Gay Kelleway on Faldal in the closing handicap.

By the time we reached Royal Ascot, Frankie had already got plenty of winners under his belt, and satisfaction enough to take a look at himself with Alastair Down.

They say that by the age of forty you get the face you deserve, and with some Flat jockeys every ounce hard-wasted down the years can exact a high toll on the wrinkle front. But at 39 the father of five that is Frankie Dettori wears it well and looks remarkably similar to the teenager who rode his first Royal Ascot winner twenty years ago next week.

'That was Markofdistinction,' Dettori recalls, 'and he was the real pioneer horse for me. He gave me my first Listed win at Lingfield then, next season, my first Group 2 at Sandown, the Queen Anne at Royal Ascot and then my first Group 1 in the Queen Elizabeth II at the Ascot festival. Big horse for me.'

Ascot has been hugely important to Dettori. History and racing folklore will always major on that still stunning afternoon in 1996 when by riding all seven winners he joyously melted down everybody's idea of what it was possible for any one man to achieve on a racecourse in a single afternoon.

But the word Ascot is marbled through Dettori's backbone just as the legend Blackpool can be found all the way through a stick of seaside rock. Royal Ascot in particular is his stamping ground, with no meeting complete without that half-cocky cocking of his head towards the appreciative stands as he slots one home first. There is no arrogance to it, but the gesture says: 'You know this is my place and I know you know this is my place.'

Historically, it has usually been a fruitful five days for Godolphin and Dettori is quick to point out that one year he rode seven winners at the meeting when it was just a four-day gig rather than the fractionally overblown five of today.

The Ascot winning post can be found at the Dettori home and Fujiyama Crest, the seventh wonder of that famous afternoon, found his way to Castello Dettori as a pet. Probably just ahead of a consortium of bookmakers who thought he might make a decent dinner.

So what does Dettori make of the now not-so-new track? He answers: 'Well, it is more fair. When you come round that home bend the straight is 75 yards longer, and if you think that does not sound a lot then, believe me, it is.

'In the old days if you were not bang up there you couldn't win. It was more tactical and much more cut-throat. Mind you, you are always going to have a maximum field for the Ascot Stakes and that is always going to be rough.'

The straight course is the subject of much debate among pundits and punters alike. Front-runners seem to get reeled in more than of old, while Polytrack winners thrive on it. Dettori says: 'Before the redevelopment you had the road to cross over and there were far more undulations. Now it is a slicker and quicker course and much less stiff than it used to be.

'As for the new stands, well let's face it, the old place had charm but it was getting a bit tired. But there is one thing I do miss and that is the walk to the paddock. You had to fight your way there but you felt like a boxer walking into the ring. No young kid having his first ride there would ever forget it.'

We are so used to Dettori's trademark celebrations that we forget the degree to which he, single-handed, changed our perception of how jockeys could behave on course. 'Look, I'm a happy-go-lucky person,' he says: 'The story of how I'm feeling is in my face. When I first came along Lester had just retired and we had Pat Eddery, who looked as miserable as Lester!

'And there was a huge row when I did a flying dismount after Mark Of Esteem won the Guineas, people asking if I had broken the rules

and complaints I had dismounted in the wrong place. And that was 1996 – not even fifteen years ago. I wasn't making things up, just showing what my character was all about, and the public loved me for it.'

It is partly the bond Dettori has forged with racegoers and partly the natural showman in him, but he has strong views on engaging the racing public. He says: 'We have to sell racing as a package and we need to get the basics right, such as an easily recognisable start to the season and a major climax to end it.

'We simply have to make it more friendly because if you've got no people you've got no sport. Admission prices are complete robbery, and that is just for the basics. You have to pay extra to go into the bit where nobody is – the members. The trial of letting people in for free was a great idea, because if you keep getting young people in eventually they will get the hang of it.'

If there is one particular area in which Dettori has been fortunate it is that there have been a number of older friends and benefactors who have taken the trouble to get the hang of him and, certainly in his younger, more impetuous days, to do some of the thinking for him. The once trendy mystical philosopher George Gurdjieff wrote a tome entitled Meetings With Remarkable Men, and Dettori could do the same with Sheikh Mohammed, Luca Cumani, John Gosden and Barney Curley, big players in his life.

And there have been days when it wasn't all broad grins and flying dismounts. He says: 'Back in the early 1990s when I had lost the job with Luca and blown a huge job in Hong Kong, that was when things were bad. John Gosden picked me up and that was an important part of me growing up as he was a great man as well as a great man to work for.

'And then one day he told me Sheikh Mohammed wanted my opinion on Balanchine, who was one of just four horses he had out in the desert in Dubai. I went and rode her work and told Sheikh Mohammed she would not be out of the frame in the Guineas. He was so pleased he nearly kissed me!' Weeks later Balanchine was beaten a short head by Las Meninas in the One Thousand Guineas, but proved herself remarkable and gave Godolphin a rocket-powered boost by winning the Oaks and then famously beating the colts in the Irish Derby.

Cumani, Gosden and the Sheikh have all had the regard and affection for Dettori to juggle the differing roles of friend, boss and father-figure. Doubtless he has tried their patience on occasions down the years but don't ever doubt his gratitude for their loyalty.

A less expected ally has been the genuinely enigmatic Curley. Dettori recalls: 'Many years ago, when I was seventeen or eighteen, there was a programme on Channel 4 at about midnight called After Dark, a discussion show for people who couldn't sleep! I came in from a night out and there was McCririck and a couple of others sitting there on the TV talking a load of rubbish. But there was this guy, sitting there quietly, who would chip in every now and again and say something which was quite outstanding.

'That was Barney, and I was drawn to him like a magnet. A month later I was at Tatts for the sales and as I walked round he called out to me. He said, "I want you to ride one for me next week. Don't tell your agent, just tell him not to book you a ride in that race."

'I was duly declared to ride and he told me he wouldn't be coming racing but that Declan Murphy would be down at the start with the horse as he was a bit of a boyo. The horse duly won and we became friends.

'When you are young, as I was, there is nothing better than having a person like Barney to talk to. And he wasn't interested in me because I rode well, but because he cared about me. I don't ride for him much now because I would kill his price, but I was good value when I was a 5lb claimer. He is still wonderfully funny company.'

Heading for his fortieth birthday in December, Dettori is in terrific mental and physical nick and shows no signs of stopping. He points out: 'Mick Kinane went on until fifty and I have plenty of ambitions left. I want to beat Lester's 470 European Group winners and ride 3,000 winners in Britain.'

A few years ago you certainly wouldn't have found him riding six at Folkestone on a Monday as he did this week. He senses he is in a good rhythm this season and, after 104 winners last year, is on schedule for his target of 150.

He says: 'I am riding horses for Mark Johnston and I work for a man who just loves his racing. How many others would have gone on from Oaks day at Epsom to watch a maiden run at Goodwood in the evening?' One of the Frankie staples has bitten the dust, however: the Ferrari has gone.

He laughs: 'The last one was too fast. It was basically a racing car – a steering wheel, a seat and a fire extinguisher. Carpets? You are joking! I thought I'd better sell this or I will kill myself. And, anyway, the world is in crisis and so we will sit the fast cars out for a bit.'

Whether any of the five Dettori offspring follow in dad's footsteps remains to be seen.

Ten-year-old Leo already takes the same size in shoes as his father but he may go down the pony-racing road, and Frankie and Catherine's three daughters are all pony mad. Then comes Rocco, the youngest, and Frankie says: 'He has a physique like a bantamweight - muscles and a six-pack. What's more, he is fearless, and he is still only five.'

This week Dettori will be donning top hat and tails for the meeting that has done so much for him and to which he has brought great lungs full of fresh air down the years.

'I'm a great believer in the tradition of it all and after racing I go off for a glass of champagne and a sandwich in the car park. Mind you, I have to take care as there are 80,000 women on course waiting to attack me!' By all accounts, in his youth he would have been happy to take the 80,000 on and he certainly seems in a good place now. He says: 'There have been three stages with me. First you start with your dreams, then you fulfil your dreams, and now I can just enjoy the pressure being off. You cannot buy experience – you panic less and the occasion never makes you jump the rails. The big days don't rattle you at all – they are the ones you look forward to.'

Ascot produced a brilliant late-finishing Royal Hunt Cup victory on Invisible Man and a fifth Godolphin Ribblesdale Stakes victory with Hibaayeb. If not quite making the planned 150 total, Dettori kicked home 133 winners in Britain alone and in September steered the filly Khawlah home at Newmarket to give Godolphin their 1,000th success in Britain.

Even more significantly he confirmed his status as the world's greatest ever global jockey when he won the Breeders' Cup Turf for Brian Meehan at Churchill Downs and within 24 hours celebrated something very special with Godolphin. Bruce Jackson was on hand.

Frankie Dettori made it a transatlantic big-race double and hoisted his 100th Group/Grade 1 winner for Godolphin yesterday when Rio De La Plata bagged the Premio Roma GBI Racing at Capannelle.

After winning the Breeders' Cup Turf on Dangerous Midge in Kentucky on Saturday, Dettori grabbed just three hours' sleep on the overnight flight to Italy before notching the landmark century for his retainer.

Dettori said: 'It's absolutely unbelievable. My first one was Balanchine in the Oaks of 1994, and it has been a great journey.

'I'm talking to you from the racecourse restaurant, having a glass of champagne to celebrate.

'I'm absolutely shattered, but I would like to stress that Rio is my favourite horse. I would have got here to ride him even if I was dead, because I love the horse.'

The Saeed bin Suroor-trained five-year-old hit the front entering the final furlong and stayed on well to record a two-and-a-half length victory over last year's winner Voila Ici.

Diana Cooper, representing Godolphin, said: 'That was a fabulous performance from Rio De La Plata and the horse really is going from strength to strength. He travelled supremely well and nothing was ever going to beat him today.

'It was fantastic for Frankie to get his 100th Group 1 winner for Godolphin in such emphatic style. Everyone at Godolphin is delighted; it is a tremendous achievement.'

Dangerous Midge lands the 2010 Breeders' Cup Turf at Churchill Downs.

Dettori reached the milestone on his 547th ride in a top-flight race, having started on Balanchine and quickly followed by the partnership winning the Irish Derby three weeks later.

Rio De La Plata has now contributed three of Dettori's 100, having won the Prix Jean-Luc Lagardere, which made him ante-post favourite for the Two Thousand Guineas, before making it 99 for Dettori in Italy last month.

Dettori's most prolific years at the top level for Godolphin came in 1999 and 2001, when he posted thirteen wins both years.

The century includes seventeen European Classics, while he has won three Prix de l'Arc de Triomphe and four King George VI and Queen Elizabeth Stakes for Godolphin.

As he turned forty in December 2010, Frankie Dettori appeared to be in a better place than any jockey in history. When he began 2011 with a One Thousand Guineas success for Godolphin on Blue Bunting it was hard to imagine that the wheels were beginning to work loose.

An unhappy ride in the Oaks on the same filly ended with a ten-day ban for easing off at the finish. Then his frantic, 24-whip-crack efforts

The Dubai Sheema Classic, 2011 – a towering performance from Rewilding.

A barnstorming Blue Bunting wins the 2011 One Thousand Guineas.

to win the Prince of Wales's Stakes for Godolphin on Rewilding were rewarded with another nine-day ban and, much more tragically, he then took a heavy fall when the same horse fell fatally early in the straight in Ascot's King George VI and Queen Elizabeth Stakes.

And even though he and Blue Bunting did link up again to win the Yorkshire Oaks, his British total was down to 72, and come the 2012 season it seemed pretty clear that the situation for Dettori at Godolphin was anything but unchallenged. In April, Lee Mottershead struck the right note.

The Italian, the Brazilian and the Frenchman are today back home in Britain. They are the three musketeers, one for all and all for one, and yet in sport that can never be wholly the truth.

Frankie Dettori, Silvestre de Sousa and Mickael Barzalona have been brought together by one master. Their wages are paid by Godolphin but they do not ride solely for Sheikh Mohammed. They also ride for themselves.

Jenson Button and Lewis Hamilton both drive for McLaren but to each the biggest rival is the other. Competition between team-mates is good for the individuals and the team. At Kempton today, the battle for bragging rights begins.

All three riders will be in action but only two will have mounts for Godolphin. De Sousa, as the man who misses out, will have to impress on horses trained by former boss Mark Johnston. The Sao Paulo import will know that, up against the stable's long-established riding superstar and a Derby-winning teenager fuelled by victory in the world's richest race, it is he who must fight hardest to be seen. Barzalona, seven days on from the vertical salute that marked his Dubai World Cup triumph aboard Monterosso, is the one with the wind beneath his wings.

Looking back there is a sad inevitability at how events progressed, a sense that Frankie was raging against an outgoing tide. We hadn't even got to June before speculation was in full spate. Racing Post *news editor Tony Smurthwaite had the story.*

Frankie Dettori last night scotched suggestions that he was slipping down the pecking order at Godolphin and put to rest brief speculation that he was ready to announce his retirement.

Without a ride in the Investec Derby on Saturday and overlooked in favour of Mickael Barzalona for the ride on Godolphin's Kailani in tomorrow's Investec Oaks, Dettori came out fighting about his future.

'Mickael got the ride in the Oaks on the word of the boss [Sheikh Mohammed] and Mahmood Al Zarooni. Nevertheless, I then got a call from Coolmore asking if I could ride in the Oaks. The boss said I could if I wanted to. As it happened nothing came of it but it shows I'm in demand.'

Dettori has ridden more than 900 winners for Godolphin and said he was more than keen to reach 1,000.

'I've got at least five more years in me,' he added. 'I'm only 41 and would challenge any jockey to a one-on-one.'

The Derby-winning rider did confess to being disappointed at having to head to Haydock on Saturday, but added: 'Life doesn't stop at the Derby.'

As to his role at Godolphin alongside first-season appointments Barzalona and Silvestre de Sousa, Dettori echoed the view from

racing manager Simon Crisford that he was the team's senior rider.

'I'm a soldier in a team,' Dettori added. 'I do what I'm told. The boss has the power to decide who rides and I've been a good soldier for the past eighteen years.'

A Twitter report last night that Dettori was ready to quit was swiftly denounced as a spoof, and the jockey added: 'All this talk of retirement and pecking orders is baffling to me and has come out of the blue. I'm quite surprised and you can be sure when I retire it will be decided by me.'

Frankie may have been defiant, but there was little doubt that Mickael Barzalona was the new kid on the Godolphin block. So few moments in that season or any other, have bettered Frankie's Ascot Gold Cup victory against his rival. The old wolf could still make his kill – as Alastair Down reflected.

There is no relief as sweet as the lifting of a siege and, like famous old actor knights treading the boards of a favourite stage, Frankie Dettori and Godolphin roared out of the doldrums with a dramatic Gold Cup one-two at Ascot yesterday.

Dettori has the winning post from the old Ascot racecourse at his home but he knows exactly where the new one is too. He took it up on Colour Vision just over a furlong from home and you could almost write the sub-plots involved in the final pulsating 200 yards as the man trying to run him down was Mickael Barzalona on his old ally Opinion Poll.

For years seemingly beyond count Frankie has been first choice for Godolphin, but this year the tea leaves have become trickier to read. Sheikh Mohammed is a ferocious competitor as well as the sport's principal benefactor, but he has never been averse to injecting a degree of competition into the lives of those who work for him, just to keep everyone on their toes.

His recruitment of Barzalona to share the Godolphin rides has had plenty of pundits assuming Dettori's days as kingpin were numbered. But after this triumph Sheikh Mohammed said: 'I am not worried about what people write – Frankie is great, but this year there is a younger man coming up.'

The Godolphin message seems clear – it's about reinvigorating the team, not redrawing the batting order. But when Dettori found Barzalona coming to nail him in the final furlong every last ounce of his fighting instincts seemed to come into play. Headed with 150 yards to run, Colour Vision edged left in the heat of battle and bumped into Opinion Poll twice.

Colour Vision dug hard in answer to Dettori's efforts and regained the lead with just 75 yards left of the two-and-a-half-mile slog, although he was palpably on top close home. There could have been no finer way for Dettori to prove that despite the threat of a serious young lion he is still king of the jungle.

I imagine as they went into the stewards' enquiry Frankie said: 'Mickael, you don't speak much English – take it from me, this isn't the time to learn.'

This was the Dettori Ascot knows and has long loved. Few sportsmen can have had a venue that has become a second home to them to the degree that Ascot has for Dettori. This place is marbled through his soul.

But jockeys thrive on winners and confidence. Frankie has had a distinctly thin time of it recently and he walked in here yesterday without a victory from 41 rides over the last three weeks.

As the old sages will tell you: 'Form is temporary, class is permanent.' Only last week I sent Dettori a text saying I was getting tired of reading his obituaries from those who have been dead-and-burying him. But you can't keep someone of his sheer ability down and the initial 'L' before his name stands for Lazarus every bit as much as it does for Lanfranco.

And Dettori remains a very important player. Jockeys and Flat racing have never had a public face that gets within furlongs of what he has brought to the sport.

This was crucial for Godolphin too. Their whole operation is about being serious players in the biggest races worldwide, and the fact that their last British Group 1 winner was Poet's Voice in September 2010 tells you that they have not been punching their weight.

The hyper-critical will say that winning the Gold Cup doesn't matter and the great middle-distance races are where the power lies. But the Gold Cup matters plenty to their arch rivals at Ballydoyle, and for Sheikh Mohammed to stand with his troops in the winner's enclosure sends out the message they may have had a few batterings but they are still in the game.

Certainly I have rarely seen them all so chuffed, and Saeed bin Suroor was in danger of floating off into the ether, he was so happy. The crowd loved it too, because to them the sight of Dettori in flight is infectiously joyous and one of the things they come to see.

Sheikh Mohammed has a country to run, which is more than can be said for anyone else at Ascot yesterday, and so he can't spend half his time banging the heads of his racing team together. Having two trainers and two jockeys does some of the re-energising for him and introduces a bit of fizz. It may help kick-start the process of making the operation leaner and meaner.

*Carrying the Olympic torch at Ascot,
2012.*

This was Godolphin's fifth Gold Cup, and they more than anyone played the major role in stopping this wonderful old race's decline – they made it fashionable again.

What's more, with less than a length covering the first three home it was a fabulous spectacle and a reminder that there will always be something marvellous and imperishable about our version of the marathon.

For Frankie there were other highlights. In July he was back at Ascot to carry the Olympic torch in front of 10,000 people. In August he finally landed the Ebor, the one big handicap that had eluded him, on Godolphin's Willing Foe. In September he won the Irish Champion Stakes on Ed Dunlop's remarkable mare Snow Fairy.

But the tide was definitely running out. Frankie's winning total barely reached fifty for the season, and when the St Leger had come round it was Barzalona who rode the Godolphin winner Encke, with Dettori gritting his teeth as he was led in third on the John Gosden-trained Michelangelo.

Then the bombshell. Unwanted by Godolphin in the Prix de l'Arc
de Triomphe, Frankie announced that he was accepting the ride on
Camelot for arch-rivals Coolmore. Where on earth was he heading now?
Julian Muscat offered calm analysis.

Perhaps it was inevitable. Months of unrest at having his wings
clipped finally rose to the surface when Frankie Dettori accepted the
Arc ride on Camelot. A race that was running out of storylines is now
likely to contain some stunning repercussions.

This is the same Dettori who said he'd made 'a mistake' when
partnering Scorpion to victory for the same Camelot connections
in the 2005 St Leger. His public lament drew a good-natured
rebuke from John Magnier after he described Coolmore as 'the
opposition'.

'Frankie, we love you and we forgive you, because you know not
what you say,' Magnier said in a rare speech at the Cartier Awards
two months later.

Does Dettori know what he is doing this time? There can be no
doubt. His expression of angst in the St Leger postscript – after
Mickael Barzalona rode Godolphin's Encke to victory, with Dettori

*Sheer delight – and a startled partner
– after Snow Fairy's triumph in the
Irish Champion Stakes.*

third aboard John Gosden's Michelangelo – told of a man near the end of his tether.

That St Leger body-blow followed on from Dettori watching as Barzalona won the Dubai World Cup on Monterosso and then sitting out the Derby and Oaks, in which Barzalona rode Kailani for Godolphin. Whatever strife his decision to ride Camelot will cause, he was not prepared to be benched for a first Arc in 25 years.

Many will wonder who could blame him. With Dettori now 'sharing' rides with Barzalona and Silvestre de Sousa, his equine arsenal has been significantly reduced. Whatever has been agreed in the background, taking the Camelot ride could provoke an employer who has not bought a yearling by any Coolmore sire since 2005 – the year Dettori won the St Leger aboard Scorpion.

This may come to be seen as the beginning of the end of a relationship that has endured since Sheikh Mohammed recruited Dettori in 1994. The days of the lucrative retainer may soon be no more. And what of Joseph O'Brien, who cannot make the 8st 11lb Camelot is due to carry? O'Brien's days in a Flat saddle are surely limited. The teenager who could not walk straight under a 6ft bridge is probably still growing.

With Joseph not the long-term solution at Ballydoyle and Dettori's bridge with Godolphin burning, speculation is bound to twin the two protagonists. Dettori has set rolling a ball that may take out several skittles before it comes to rest. In the Arc three years ago he was legged aboard the sheikh's Cavalryman by Andre Fabre. Much has changed: there was no place for Dettori aboard Fabre's Masterstroke this time round.

Dettori could seal his fate were Camelot to deny Masterstroke on Sunday. The most striking thing is he appears to be contemplating that possibility with his eyes wide open.

The racing world was agog. Camelot and Frankie finished seventh in the Arc. But where was he heading now? Lee Mottershead addressed the burning question.

In a sense it did not matter whether Frankie Dettori and Camelot finished first or seventh in yesterday's Qatar Prix de l'Arc de

Before mounting Camelot for the 2012 Arc – Frankie in the colours of Derrick Smith, one of the big hitters for Coolmore.

Triomphe. The pivotal point in this tale came on Wednesday when Dettori stunned the racing world by deciding to partner the Coolmore-owned colt. Long before we went to Longchamp the damage had been done.

It is now difficult to imagine that Dettori will begin next year as a Godolphin jockey. It is also hard to believe that Dettori was not aware his decision to team up with Sheikh Mohammed's fiercest rival must severely jeopardise his association with Godolphin. One therefore has to ask the question why he did it.

What is absolutely beyond doubt is that it was not expected. Last Monday this newspaper spoke at length with Dettori, framing a piece around his quest to secure a 25th consecutive ride in the Arc. At that stage we knew Camelot was without a jockey but, given the furore that followed his 2005 St Leger success on Scorpion, it seemed nonsensical to even hint at the possibility of a reunion seven years down the line. By agreeing to join forces with John Magnier's team at Longchamp, Dettori astounded everyone.

It is understood that no permission was sought by Dettori and also that he used a text message to inform Godolphin bosses of his agreement to partner Camelot. The surprise with which they greeted the news will have been matched by disappointment.

In Dettori's defence, there was absolutely no contractual obligation on him to request any sort of approval from Godolphin. It can therefore be argued that he has done nothing wrong. Had he ridden Snow Fairy, as was once expected, there would not have been a story, but Godolphin and Sheikh Mohammed will feel that by signing up to 'the other side' their jockey has committed an act of disloyalty and broken the code of honour the Maktoums hold dear.

The two sides have been good for each other, both serving the other's cause admirably over nearly two decades. However, by consenting to ride the colt Aidan O'Brien describes as the best he has trained, Dettori, paid a vast retainer by Godolphin, effectively agreed to help Coolmore's bid to boost the value of Montjeu's replacement, a soon-to-be Coolmore stallion who will be competing for business with Sheikh Mohammed's Darley stallions. As such Sheikh Mohammed will feel Dettori has divorced himself from the team cause.

Dettori knew how his boss would interpret his actions because he had already committed what he himself concluded to be a misguided act.

Following the interview he gave to Racing UK at Salisbury on Wednesday it was obvious he had insisted on not being asked the difficult question everyone wanted to hear answered. In an interview conducted seven years earlier he had faced the questions that Nick Luck surely longed to pose.

During an appearance on BBC Radio 5 Live in the days after Scorpion's St Leger he was asked by Simon Mayo if he would again ride for Ballydoyle.

'No,' he said. 'It's like Michael Schumacher one day driving for Ferrari and then driving another car. It left a bit of a sour taste with everybody, so perhaps I shouldn't have done it. They are our main rivals and you can't be black one day and then white another day. I made a winning mistake but it doesn't reflect well on my team when they see me ride for the main opposition. You learn by your mistakes.'

In Dettori's defence his situation has changed greatly since 2005. This is the year in which he has found himself fighting with a young rival for Sheikh Mohammed's affections.

A fine example of the flying dismount – this time from Goodwood Mirage at Newmarket in October 2012.

Dettori's top-dog status has been challenged to the extent that one could make a persuasive case for saying he has been placed in an impossible position. It was Mickael Barzalona who wore the Godolphin blue when winning this year's Dubai World Cup and Ladbrokes St Leger, while it was Barzalona who was selected over Dettori for important mounts in some of the year's other key races.

A senior figure close to Dettori admitted last month that his friend was not finding the situation easy to handle. It is therefore possible that Dettori, seeking a way out of Godolphin, viewed his Arc booking as a premeditated way of forcing Sheikh Mohammed's hand. More likely his actions were reflective of a committed sportsman, still arguably the finest pound-for-pound rider in the sport, attempting to remind the world he remains the best in the business.

Top sportsmen on occasions have to be blinkered and selfish. Perhaps for Dettori, his ego massaged by overtures from an

On Ikhtisas, Newmarket, October 2012.

admiring and slightly mischievous suitor, this was one such occasion.

It would not be a seismic shock if Dettori is offered a more regular role with Ballydoyle, for whom he would be a thrilling appointment. Given Joseph O'Brien's weight situation, Magnier must surely now consider asking Dettori to become Ballydoyle's big-race jockey, a job that would allow Dettori to remain in Newmarket. The lure of another chunky retainer and a plethora of Group 1 opportunities might be irresistible to someone who is not only an outstanding jockey but also one of the sport's finest assets.

Now, though, could be the time for a change. Some of Dettori's senior weighing-room colleagues have long envied his close relationship with Sheikh Mohammed. Few men have been seen to cuddle the sheikh in public. Dettori is one such man but the embracing days are now almost certainly over.

On the day Dettori's booking for Camelot was revealed, Sheikh Mohammed was active on Twitter. One of his tweets now seems particularly relevant. He wrote: 'When a leader always leads by example in everything, his employees can never ignore these silent messages.'

Godolphin's founder, rightly or wrongly, will feel he has led by example. It will come as a surprise if his highest-paid employee does not discover in the near future that silent messages are followed by decisive action.

A fortnight later, the story bowed to the inevitable, as Lee reported.

The shattering of a union that once seemed unshakable was revealed yesterday when Godolphin and Frankie Dettori announced that one of the most successful and durable associations in the history of sport is coming to an end, with the two sides set to part amicably at the end of the year.

Speculation that Dettori's sensational decision to partner the Coolmore-owned Camelot in the Qatar Prix de l'Arc de Triomphe could trigger the end of his eighteen-year tenure as Sheikh Mohammed's principal rider was proved accurate when racingpost.com broke the news that the world's most famous jockey will continue his glittering career as a freelance in 2013.

In a prepared statement that employed carefully chosen words, Godolphin racing manager Simon Crisford stated the stable had come to the conclusion that Dettori's retainer 'was not really working', but underlined that a mutual decision had been reached, the 41-year-old jockey describing himself as in need of 'a new challenge'. With Dettori gone, Mickael Barzalona, triumphant for Godolphin in this year's Dubai World Cup and St Leger, is to receive unofficial promotion to the position of number-one jockey to the organisation, which for the second year running will retain both him and Silvestre de Sousa. Confusion over Barzalona's status within Godolphin relative to Dettori had led to gossip, with Dettori thought to have become frustrated at seeing a colleague initially installed as his understudy posting major triumphs on Monterosso, Encke and next year's QIPCO One Thousand Guineas favourite Certify.

In his own statement Dettori added : 'I have ridden some great horses and it is difficult to pick out individual moments because the whole eighteen years have been a highlight. But Dubai Millennium is still the best horse I have ridden, while Balanchine gave me my first Classic win and Lammtarra was also an exceptional horse.'

Dettori, second for Godolphin in an Italian Group 1 yesterday, became inextricably linked with Sheikh Mohammed during a near two-decade association in which they combined to land most of the sport's major events. For Godolphin, Dettori rode the winners of nine British Classics, four King George VI and Queen Elizabeth Stakes, three Prix de l'Arc de Triomphe and three Dubai World Cups. In addition, he successfully teamed up with numerous non-Godolphin horses who ran under Sheikh Mohammed's control, notably when lifting the 2008 Breeders' Cup Classic on the John Gosden-trained Raven's Pass. Dettori has a strike-rate of 28 per cent for Godolphin, having partnered 943 winners from 3,423 rides, including 372 Stakes races. He has ridden for Godolphin at 65 different racecourses in fourteen countries, winning at 55 of those tracks.

At the very best this could be described as a career setback. But mid-November brought something much worse: public disgrace, in the form of the revelation by the French racing authority France Galop that Dettori had failed a drugs test at Longchamp on Arc trials day in September. The inevitable ban was reported by Scott Burton, our man in France, on 6 December.

Frankie Dettori has expressed his determination to rebuild his reputation after yesterday being banned for six months for what French racing authorities described as a serious breach of the rules regarding prohibited substances.

In a statement released by his solicitor Christopher Stewart-Moore, the three-time champion jockey accepted full responsibility for the offence and acknowledged that he had let down the sport, his fans and his family.

The suspension, which will be reciprocated worldwide, is backdated to the declaration of Dettori's 'medical ineligibility' to ride by a panel of French doctors on 20 November, meaning he will be free to return on 20 May, 2013, eleven days before the Investec Oaks at Epsom.

In the statement, Dettori stressed that the impact on both his private life and his public reputation is of at least equal importance to him as any perceived damage to his hitherto glittering career in the saddle.

'He told me he fully accepts France Galop's decision,' said Stewart-Moore. 'He also accepts that he has let down the sport he loves and all those involved with it, as well as the wider public. But most of all – and this is his greatest regret – he has let down his wife and children.'

Neither Dettori's statement, nor the press release from France Galop, made any specific reference to the substance found in his system during routine testing at Longchamp on 16 September, but his team have made no effort to refute widespread reports that the positive test was for cocaine.

'Frankie could make excuses – he has, after all, regularly been tested for prohibited substances throughout his career,' Stewart-Moore added. 'He is clear, however, that the responsibility for his current situation lies squarely with him. From the start of France Galop's inquiry he has acknowledged to them that he made a mistake and that the fault was his.'

France Galop is sticking to its policy of not releasing details of the substance on grounds of medical confidentiality.

Dettori, who was cautioned by the Metropolitan Police for possession of cocaine in 1993, holds a unique position in being unquestionably racing's most widely recognised figure outside the sport. The repercussions of his ban will therefore travel far beyond the racing pages, a fact acknowledged in his press release.

Stewart-Moore said: 'Racing has been good to Frankie and he knows that his privileged position brings with it responsibility. For this reason he is determined to rebuild his reputation when he returns to the saddle in six months' time.'

He added: 'He is enormously grateful for all the opportunities he has been given by owners and trainers over the years and for the support of his many fans.'

Dettori split from Godolphin, his employers of eighteen years, in October towards the end of a difficult season with Sheikh Mohammed's operation during which he was frequently asked to play second fiddle to newly retained rider Mickael Barzalona. The

This way in: Frankie about to enter the Big Brother house.

split came shortly after Dettori's decision to take the ride aboard Camelot in the Prix de l'Arc de Triomphe for Godolphin's chief rivals Coolmore.

The backdating of the suspension reflects favourably on the co-operation Dettori's team have provided to France Galop throughout the process. Backdating bans has not always been done in previous cases and the extra month it will afford Dettori as he seeks to establish himself as one of racing's most highly sought-after freelances could prove invaluable.

Richard Hughes ended 2012 as champion jockey despite being prevented from starting his season until 2 May after serving a fifty-day suspension imposed by Indian stewards for not riding to orders, although Dettori finds himself in a different position from Hughes as he is without a powerful retainer on which to base his comeback.

France Galop made no secret of how seriously it takes the offence in its statement, ordering Dettori to give fresh samples for testing before his return.

'Given the grave nature of the breach of the rules of racing, the jockey is ordered to present himself before a doctor authorised by the medical commission as of 20 April 2013,' France Galop said.

The French authority also stated its expectation that the ban would be adhered to by 'horseracing authorities worldwide for all races under their ruling.'

There are many ways to set about rebuilding a damaged reputation – some more unusual than others. Two days after that report, the Racing Post *revealed that the jockey was to participate in a New Year edition of* Celebrity Big Brother, *the 'reality' television programme in which 'housemates' live together completely cut off from the outside world.*

If 2012 had been a momentous year in the rollercoaster career of Frankie Dettori, 2013 would begin in the most bizarre circumstances.

SALVATION LINE

PREVIOUS SPREAD: Frankie's
first winner for his new employer:
Shamshon scoots clear at Sandown
Park.

However much Frankie protested to the contrary, it did not look like a good idea to the rest of us. The first thing he did in his hoped-for 'redemption' year of 2013 was to go in for Celebrity Big Brother. For three weeks he and assorted soap stars and Z-listers bumbled along the reality show trail in assorted embarrassing outfits, which for Dettori included both full pouting-lip drag and dress uniform of Italian dictator Benito Mussolini. His children loved it and he earned a thick wedge for charity. But as for convincing the racing world of a return to the big time, they remembered John McEnroe's immortal line to the tennis umpire: 'You cannot be serious!'

It was unhappily easy to believe that for Frankie the future was now behind him. It was not until the end of May that his clearance to ride again finally came through, and when the first winner duly came in early June there was as much a sense of relief as of expectation. Graham Dench was on the spot.

Frankie Dettori celebrated with a trademark flying dismount after his wait for a first winner since his return to the saddle ended at Sandown with a half-length win on Asian Trader in the 5f handicap.

He has now set himself a target of 100 winners this year.

Since returning at Epsom last Friday from the six-month suspension he received for failing a drugs test in France – a ban which had been extended by almost a fortnight through issues with a subsequent test – Dettori had managed only two modest placings from eleven rides, but Sandown offered him several live chances and he made the most of his first proper opportunity on Asian Trader, although a slow start on the habitual front-runner gave his supporters an anxious 59 seconds.

Dettori admitted relief at getting off the mark but said: 'I've ridden 3,000 winners but everyone is waiting for this.'

He added: 'The first winner is always sweet and I've had plenty of practice these last six days. I'm not aiming high, but I'd like to win 100 races now. I've got plenty of rides coming up, including ten on Saturday.'

As for the slow start and the fear of getting boxed in on the William Haggas-trained winner, Dettori said it was not a problem.

'When you're on a horse who can travel you always find room,' he said, before returning to the sanctity of the changing room.

Frankie back in the saddle – and soon ejecting the saddle, after winning on Asian Trader at Sandown Park.

For a while that first winner didn't seem to presage much of a summer, and that talk of 100 winners fell on empty air as racing seemed only anxious for Frankie to act in minor roles. Then at the start of July came the bombshell. Just as he seemed to be sliding down a snake, he found himself a gleaming new ladder –as Lee Mottershead reported.

Frankie Dettori plans to put himself and new boss Sheikh Joaan Al Thani 'on top of the world' following confirmation of a sensational new association between the sport's highest-profile individual and one of its most ambitious and powerful new owners.

Dettori, whose eighteen-year job with Sheikh Mohammed came to an end last year, has switched his allegiance from Dubai to Qatar after on Sunday agreeing a one-year deal with an owner who describes the former Godolphin stable jockey as his 'idol'.

Such reverence, however, has not been enough to get Dettori on the QIPCO Sussex Stakes-bound Toronado, who, like the other Sheikh Joaan-owned horses with Richard Hannon, will continue to be ridden by champion jockey Richard Hughes.

Dettori returned to the saddle on 31 May after serving a six-month suspension for testing positive for cocaine, but his comeback has so far yielded only five winners, none of which came at Royal Ascot, where the 42-year-old rode two horses for Sheikh Joaan, a cousin of Sheikh Fahad.

Like Sheikh Fahad, Sheikh Joaan has proved willing to spend freely, his purchases having included Toronado, his Group 1-winning stablemate Olympic Glory, Poule d'Essai des Poulains winner Style Vendome, and two-year-old filly Sandiva, who was sold by her syndicate owners for a reputed £1 million before her well-beaten second under Dettori in the Albany Stakes.

'Sheikh Joaan is now a big player in racing,' said Dettori, who yesterday drew a blank from two rides at Wolverhampton. 'He is keen to expand and I can see the passion and love for racing he has. He has lots of top quality horses and I'm looking forward to riding them all. He's the sort of person you want to work with, so I'm delighted to be with him'

'I'm looking forward to the future and Sheikh Joaan could possibly be one of the best owners in the world. I want to use my experience to give him as much success as I can.

'My plan is for us to have a long-term relationship and for us to be very successful together. He is a very nice man and a very ambitious man. I don't really know him that well but all big owners want big winners, and that's what he wants.'

Asked if he was disappointed to be passed over for the Goodwood ride on Toronado, Dettori added: 'I'm looking at the big picture, which is to build a proper racing stable for Sheikh Joaan. I'm looking to five and ten years down the line. It's not just about the Sussex

Stakes. I'm looking at putting Sheikh Joaan and myself on the top of the racing world. That's the vision.'

Sheikh Joaan's assistant Sian Jones revealed the deal had been finalised on Sunday at Chantilly, where her employer met both Dettori and Richard Hannon junior.

'Sheikh Joaan had wanted this for a long time,' said Jones. 'Everyone has their idol and Frankie is Sheikh Joaan's. He had a few words with Frankie before he rode Mshawish for him at Ascot and after that decided he wanted to go ahead with the deal.

'We drew up the contract, met with Frankie at Chantilly and got everything signed and sealed. The first contract is for a year. At the end of the season he'll ride for us in Qatar and Dubai, and if both teams are happy we'll carry on.

'Sheikh Joaan feels Frankie is a true horseman who can get the best out of a horse. He has ridden so many Group 1 winners all over the world and His Excellency feels that by signing Frankie he has the best man. We have many trainers but it's good to have one jockey on our side.'

Jones added: 'At the moment Toronado will stay with Richard Hughes in the Sussex Stakes and if the result goes well he will then continue to be ridden by Richard.

'Richard will stay in our first colours for all Richard Hannon's horses, but we have horses all over France with different trainers and in England with Marco Botti, Sir Michael Stoute and Lady Cecil, so there are plenty of good horses for Frankie.'

The first winner was in a little maiden race at Sandown. It was an ordinary day but there was no mistaking the potential of what might lie ahead. Tom Parks and Bruce Jackson filed the story.

The first of many was the message from Frankie Dettori after he began his new retainer for Sheikh Joaan Al Thani in spectacular style.

There was no flying dismount, but Shamshon made the jockey's first winner in the sheikh's colours memorable by spreadeagling his rivals in the 5f maiden.

The son of Invincible Spirit, one of ten two-year-olds owned by the sheikh with Richard Hannon, was backed in to 8-11 from evens and made all under a cool ride from Dettori.

The delighted jockey said: 'To win first time out by six lengths for my first winner in my new job is very pleasing.'

Dettori revealed that, as well as the ten with Hannon, he has some fifty two-year-olds, spread across four or five trainers, to partner across the Channel.

'With the way the two-year-old programme is in France their races are later in the season,' he said. 'Everyone has been getting in a panic about my quiet summer but not me with these two-year olds to look forward to.'

Another big-race mount is Treve, winner of the Prix de Diane, and Dettori heads to Chantilly on Tuesday morning, before riding at Deauville, to partner the Criquette Head-Maarek-trained filly.

Dettori added: 'Criquette says the Vermeille and Arc are definites, and she has not said no to the Nonette.'

Treve was something to look forward to and when she finally reappeared in September she did not disappoint – as Isabel Matthew wrote from Longchamp.

Frankie Dettori returned to the big time as the unbeaten Treve earned him his first Group 1 success since his return to the saddle from a six-month drugs ban with a brilliant victory in the Qatar Prix Vermeille.

Dettori can now dream of a record-equalling fourth Prix de l'Arc de Triomphe success on Sheikh Joaan Al Thani's flying filly, who evoked memories of 2008 Vermeille and Arc heroine Zarkava in eclipsing her rivals by a length and three-quarters.

It was not all plain sailing for the three-year-old, who under Dettori's confident ride had to overcome trouble in running before seeing off the Lady Cecil-trained Wild Coco in the closing stages, having been trapped on the rail at the entrance to the home straight.

Winning the 2013 Prix Vermeille on the great Treve – and (opposite) with Sheikh Joaan after the race.

It was an emotional triumph for trainer Criquette Head-Maarek, who said: 'They didn't go very fast and to do what she did today she must be exceptional.

'She pulled, she was closed in on the rail and then she had to move through horses – it was a real test for her.'

A four-length winner of the Prix de Diane on her previous outing in June, the daughter of Motivator was extending her winning streak to four and surely did enough to persuade her owner to stump up €100,000 to supplement her to the Arc.

With soft underfoot conditions, Treve put paid to any stamina doubts to give Sheikh Joaan, who appointed Dettori his retained jockey in July, a third Group 1 victory for his grey and maroon colours.

Dettori, who returned to action in May after serving his suspension for testing positive for cocaine at this course last year, said: 'I was a bit worried because of the slow pace but the plan was always to wait as long as we could.

'She has an exceptional turn of foot and I knew from riding her in work in the past couple of weeks that she was in great form.'

He added: 'If we get a good draw in the Arc she will be very competitive.'

In 1979, Head-Maarek won the Vermeille with Three Troikas before the filly went on to Arc glory, but Treve, who is now vying for favouritism for the 6 October showpiece, would be Sheikh Joaan's first runner in the contest.

The owner bought Treve in July from the Head family's Haras du Quesnay.

Frankie was back at the top of the ladder, but in the riding game you never know when the snakes might bite. The Arc was just a few days away. Then all of a sudden – as Lewis Porteous reported – it was out of sight.

Frankie Dettori's dreams of crowning his comeback with a win aboard Treve in the Qatar Prix de l'Arc de Triomphe on Sunday lay in tatters last night after the rider was ruled out for the season with a fractured right ankle sustained in a freak accident at Nottingham.

A minor fixture at Nottingham – and the Arc dream lies in tatters.

Dettori's agent Ray Cochrane said the injury was a 'disaster' for the jockey, who will be replaced by Thierry Jarnet on Treve, the unbeaten filly's trainer Criquette Head-Maarek said.

'It's really bad news for Frankie but these things happen,' Head-Maarek said.

'They go out there every day to ride and it could happen to anyone.

'[Owner] Sheikh Joaan [Al Thani] has agreed that Thierry Jarnet will be on board Treve in the Arc. He knows her really well so that won't be a problem.'

Jarnet had ridden Treve in her first three starts, including the Prix de Diane. He has also twice been successful in the Arc on Subotica in 1992 and Carnegie two years later.

Riding Eland Ally for trainer Tom Tate in the class 5 handicap over five furlongs, Dettori was unseated on his way to post shortly after leaving the parade ring.

While it may have looked a relatively soft fall, it soon became clear it was far more serious as Dettori was unable to put weight on the ankle as he tried to get to his feet.

Clearly distressed, Dettori was quickly attended to by medical staff, who wheeled the jockey by chair to the track's medical room.

'I've sprained my ankle,' Dettori shouted to his colleagues, 'get some ice ready' before disappearing out of sight.

The original prognosis by course doctor Chris Reynolds was that the injury was nothing more than 'soft tissue damage' but X-rays later confirmed the worst fears.

Cochrane said: 'Frankie has fractured his ankle. It's a disaster. He is feeling really down about it. He'll be out for at least a month and I would be surprised if he rode again this season.'

It soon became clear that riding again that season would be out of the question, and it was not until the New Year that a mounted Dettori was spotted in Newmarket. But when he was, the birdsong was definitely optimistic, as our man in HQ, David Milnes, reported.

Frankie Dettori returned to the saddle for the first time in more than three months yesterday and revealed he could be back race-riding, on the all-weather in Britain, as early as next week as he bids to put the injury that robbed him of the winning ride on Treve in last year's Prix de l'Arc de Triomphe behind him.

The former Godolphin number one, who broke his ankle in a fall from Eland Ally before the start of a race at Nottingham just four days before the Arc, received the all-clear following a scan on Monday and immediately put his fitness to the test when riding out for Jeremy Noseda in Newmarket.

The three-time champion jockey is now looking forward to resuming his duties as retained rider to Sheikh Joaan Al Thani.

In addition to Treve, whom he partnered to success in the Group 1 Prix Vermeille at Longchamp before her devastating display in the Arc, Dettori can look forward to renewing his acquaintance with other stars such as the Richard Hannon-trained Group 1 winner

Olympic Glory. Dettori said yesterday: 'It's all positive as regards returning to the saddle as the scan was clear when I had it yesterday and I was back riding out for Jeremy this morning .

'Thankfully, it went well and I didn't feel a twinge or anything from the ankle, which is the same one I broke in my plane crash fourteen years ago but on the other side.'

During the early stages of his recovery Dettori had to wear a cast and, later, a boot on his foot. He has been working hard on his fitness in recent weeks but there is one form of treatment he has not resorted to.

He said: 'I have been doing the usual things to build up my fitness including long walks, but I have yet to take up Ryan Moore's offer of a session of cryotherapy, where they put you in a chamber with a temperature of -130°C!' Rather than resume riding in Qatar or Dubai, Dettori revealed he wants to hone his fitness closer to home.

He said: 'If all goes well I would be looking to return to race-riding on the all-weather here towards the end of next week. My aim is to get going again here, but I am due to go to the King's Cup meeting in Saudi Arabia next month. After that, if Sheikh Joaan wants me to pop over to Dubai or Qatar to ride one I will, but I will be mainly based in Britain for the rest of the winter.'

In addition to the established stars, Dettori can look forward to partnering a host of big-money yearling buys in 2014 and beyond following the sheikh's purchases at Tattersalls and elsewhere last autumn, not least the unnamed Galileo sister to 2012 Oaks winner Was, now in training with Andre Fabre, who cost a record five million guineas.

She is one of around one hundred horses Dettori will ride for Sheikh Joaan's Al Shaqab Racing this year. Al Shaqab racing adviser Harry Herbert said: 'It's fantastic news that Frankie has had the all-clear after his scan as he is a key element in the team put together by Sheikh Joaan.

'I know he is excited about the season ahead and is taking it very seriously and it so happens we are going down to south-west France together in the morning to look at some of the Al Shaqab horses in training there. On the racing front, we hope to run Mshawish, who is trained by Mikel Delzangles, in a two-mile race in Qatar at the end of February, so Frankie could well ride him.'

Herbert had the pleasure of meeting Treve for the first time in the flesh at Criquette Head-Maarek's yard just before Christmas. He said: 'I hadn't seen Treve before but she looks fantastic and is wintering very well. Those around her at the yard are thrilled with how she has filled out and it's very exciting for this year.'

Reflecting on the prospect of renewing his acquaintance with Treve, Dettori said: 'It's the middle of January so it will be a while before I think about Treve, but obviously she is one of many to look forward to when I get going.'

What was first needed was a winner to put the bubbles back in the Dettori bottle. Lee Mottershead was pleased to be there when it arrived.

Rarely does a midweek winter afternoon on the Lingfield all-weather get graced by such an impressive tan.

Today, thanks to Dubai sun, the tan will get bronzer still, yet it is not just the dermatological glow that impressed but also the man who bore it. If day two of the comeback goes half as well as the first, Frankie Dettori will be delighted.

He remains the world's most famous jockey. It will take a while before he is anywhere close to being the world's fittest jockey, but his aura, charisma and talent all remain wonderfully striking. The number of extra racegoers he pulled in through Lingfield's turnstiles could have been counted on one hand, but the few who did come, not least the large group of schoolchildren, witnessed a return from injury described by its exhausted subject as 'a fairytale'.

This was not, of course, his first comeback in recent times. On 31 May last year he returned at Epsom seeking to put behind him an episode that some claimed had dented his reputation. Very quickly, however, we forgot about Celebrity Big Brother and concentrated on the re-emergence of the superstar who used to be Sheikh Mohammed's man but is now Sheikh Joaan's.

In the Sheikh Joaan colours.

Dubai was swapped for Qatar but this afternoon Dettori will be riding for Qatar in Dubai. Yesterday, he was engaged in domestic duties and did rather well, winning his first race back on Eco Warrior and his second on Gone With The Wind. The third race was never likely to be won, but not long after it had been lost Dettori and his mended ankle were being whisked to Gatwick Airport.

Aboard Eco Warrior he exquisitely made all to win a maiden that carried a first prize of £2,385.95. The Arc was worth £2,229,853.66 to the triumphant connections, of which Dettori would have been one but for the ankle. As spring turns to summer Treve will be back with Dettori in the saddle, almost certainly not blowing as much as he was here.

'I'm knackered,' he said as he dismounted from Eco Warrior. 'The adrenaline takes over in the race but when I pulled up I was paying the price. It feels fantastic, though. It's silly, but I was nervous this morning, as nervous as I would have been before a big race.'

By now he had sprayed champagne over the school kids and was in full flow, talking as engagingly as few in the weighing room can.

'This is a miracle,' he said.

'My surgeon told me I'd be back within six to nine months but I'm back after three and a half. This year I'm also starting on level terms. It's a completely different story to last year.

'I told someone in my house to throw the 2013 diary in the bin. I don't want to remember anything about it. Myself and Criquette [Head] got Treve to the Arc but the last piece in the jigsaw was the race and I didn't ride her. I'm looking forward to re-associating myself with her but that's miles away.'

More immediately, the 43-year-old – who revealed he expects Richard Hughes to retain the ride on star miler Toronado – will be racing in the desert at what was always a happy hunting ground when he had a different boss.

'It will be a bit of a choke moment when I see my old peg,' he said. 'Apparently I have a locker that hasn't been opened since 2012. I'm still the leading jockey at Meydan and I still have some good friends and good memories. I'll take those with me and enjoy it.'

After Meydan, where his two mounts include Sheikh Joaan's Mshawish, he will be back at Lingfield on Saturday, although agent Ray Cochrane has been told not to get carried away.

'I told Ray I don't want to be champion jockey,' said the three-time champion. 'I want to be selective and ride horses that have a chance. We have about seventy horses in France and around the same in England so I'll be spread between the two countries a lot. It'll be very hard to predict how many winners I'll have – but I've got one!' Soon enough he had two, thanks to Gone With The Wind, but there was no flying dismount. There perhaps might never be one again. The ankle needs protecting.

'I've been told to take it easy with that,' he said. 'It won't be until the summer and even then I don't know if I'll do it.'

The flying dismounts might be a thing of the past but, as the champagne-spraying showed, Dettori remains the supreme showman – not to mention one of the very best horsemen.

A month later the temptation once again to launch skywards from the victory saddle proved irresistible after the former English-raced Dubday had swept through to win the featured Emir's Trophy and give Sheikh Joaan a home town triumph in Qatar – as Howard Wright witnessed.

Frankie Dettori could not resist a flying dismount after he won the Emir's Trophy, the richest Thoroughbred race staged in Qatar, on the four-year-old Dubday for his new retainer Sheikh Joaan Al Thani's Al Shaqab Racing operation.

Despite being handed a health warning by his doctor after breaking his ankle in October in a fall that prevented him from taking the ride on the sheikh's Arc winner Treve, Dettori produced his trademark flourish after powering British-bred Dubday to a three-quarter-length win over Peter Anders, for the first prize of 1.14 million riyals (£187,637).

'That was great, and fantastic to do it in my new home,' Dettori said as he received the cheers of the local crowd and congratulations of his Qatari bosses. 'I'm so pleased for Sheikh Joaan because this was important.'

Sheikh Joaan purchased Dubday, a son of Dubawi, specially to run in the race after he had won his first two races in Qatar.

Dettori added: 'When Dubday put his head down and ran on for me I knew he'd catch the leader. He's a decent stayer and, if he goes to Dubai, he won't be disgraced.'

Dubday could not do the business in Dubai but as winter turned to spring Dettori and his patron's thoughts turned increasingly to the encouraging bulletins coming from Chantilly as Treve prepared for her comeback in the Prix Ganay. She was their unbeaten superstar and for Frankie she seemed his securest ticket to glittering prizes. It was not to prove so easy, as Scott Burton related.

The camps of both winner and vanquished laid claim to the best-in-the-world tag after a pulsating duel in yesterday's Prix Ganay ended with Arc heroine Treve losing her unbeaten record at the hands of Cirrus Des Aigles.

British racegoers can now look forward to both Gallic greats crossing the Channel for their next outing – and a possible rematch at Royal Ascot.

Looking ahead to Treve's planned run in the Prince of Wales's Stakes, a philosophical Frankie Dettori said: 'She'll get her ground there and is still the very best – she got beaten a short neck.'

Cirrus Des Aigles's trainer Corine Barande-Barbe, who insisted in the build-up to yesterday's Longchamp Group 1 that it would produce a 'great duel' despite bookmakers making Treve 2-5, was equally emphatic about her eight-year-old's place in the global pecking order.

'He's phenomenal and I think, today at least, he's the best in the world,' she said.

While Team Treve have a definite goal, Camp Cirrus are leaning towards the Investec Coronation Cup at Epsom on 7 June, although meeting Treve in the Prince of Wales's a week and a half later is a possibility if the gelding did not make Epsom.

Barande-Barbe added: 'His next race could be the Coronation Cup. You couldn't run there and at Royal Ascot, although he could go to Ascot later in the summer for the King George. For now I just want to enjoy this.'

Treve was pushed out to 2-1 for the Prince of Wales's by William Hill, although 6-4 was the general price, while Cirrus Des Aigles' odds were cut to between 7-2 and 9-2. Treve, eased to a general 7-2 for the Arc – Ladbrokes offered 5-1 – may have lost the sheen of invincibility but little else in defeat to a horse who long ago elevated his popular label of 'Fighting Cirrus' to something far nobler than that of a mere scrapper.

Christophe Soumillon played his hand well on the winner, refusing to chase Treve's high-class hare Belle De Crecy, instead sitting third behind Joshua Tree. Dettori spent the first half of the race in last place aboard a perfectly switched-off Treve, before moving on to the shoulder of Cirrus Des Aigles halfway around the long homeward turn.

The pair had the race to themselves throughout the final two furlongs but, hard as she tried, Treve was unable to accelerate away in the same way she had on five previous starts.

'It's a shame because you don't want to see a champion get beaten like this, through circumstances,' Dettori said. 'I had the perfect race, it was just the ground was too heavy.

'Cirrus Des Aigles was fitter, more hardened and loved the ground. My filly goes on it but on this ground she can't exploit her turn of foot. The Arc was soft, this is heavy. Take nothing away from the winner, though.'

Soon after her initial debrief with Dettori, Head-Maarek withdrew from the circle of advisers drawn from Al Shaqab Racing to speak with owner Sheikh Joaan Al Thani by telephone.

Like Dettori, she was adamant the track – which had taken 25mm of rain in the 48 hours before racing and at least two more heavy showers once the action started – was a big factor.

'She was having her comeback against a horse who had raced twice and on that ground – that made the difference,' said Head-Maarek.

'In principle she'll run at Ascot. There's no reason to change plan provided she comes out of it okay.'

The brutal nature of the Ganay was illustrated by the front pair covering the final furlong in an agonising 13.62 seconds - more than a second slower than the penultimate furlong.

Head-Maarek added: 'She lost a battle, not the war. The only thing is she has had a hard race because she's so honest.

'Cirrus Des Aigles is a fantastic horse and had the advantage of two runs behind him. On faster ground Treve will be better and she definitely needed it.'

Supportive words, yet you did not have to be a total cynic to detect some straws in the wind. Frankie continued on track, winning his first British Group 1 in two years by taking the Lockinge on Olympic Glory for Sheikh Joaan, and then gave him a Royal Ascot winner with The Wow Signal in the Coventry.

More Royal Ascot success, as The Wow Signal wins the Coventry Stakes.

But it only took a day before the worries that hung around Treve's losing battle at Longchamp were made flesh when she was an unhappy-looking third in the Prince of Wales's Stakes, under the watchful eye of Lee Mottershead.

At three, Treve was unbeatable, but at four the aura of invincibility has disappeared. Two runs have resulted in two defeats and yesterday the writing was on the wall even before she entered her her starting stall.

The stunning Arc heroine was unable to continue a wonderful Royal Ascot for owner Sheikh Joaan, who arrived at Ascot as part of the royal procession but left with a major question mark hanging over his number-one Thoroughbred after the Criquette Head-Maarek-trained 2013 horse of the year suffered her most comprehensive defeat.

Frankie Dettori, who had been in the saddle when Treve succumbed to Cirrus Des Aigles last month, felt what everyone saw in the moments leading up to the race.

The 8-13 favourite went to post appallingly, displaying an unattractive gait that was repeated in the race, in which the four-year-old – entered last week for the King George VI and Queen Elizabeth Stakes – attempted to mount a challenge early in the straight but at no point looked like threatening The Fugue.

'She went down really bad,' said Dettori. 'I was a bit worried. In the race she warmed up okay but there was a worry and I was never comfortable.

'I was following The Fugue but I was struggling to keep up with her. She didn't feel the best. It could be the ground. Who knows? Maybe she got a tweak somewhere. I was never in a comfort zone at any stage. The horse wasn't there.'

Head-Maarek said: 'Her action was not right but I don't know why. Maybe we will discover something.

'When she went down to post she didn't please me. She couldn't extend herself like she usually does. I had a problem with her feet not long ago but it looked as if everything had come back together.

'I'm going to put her in a longer race. They will go slower and maybe it will be easier for her. From three to four they change and you never know what can happen.

'We lost a battle, not the war- and you know today is the 18th of June, the anniversary of Waterloo!'

Dettori himself had a French day to remember at Deauville in August, winning both Group 1 events on the card, the Prix Morny with The Wow Signal and Prix Jean Romanet on the Newmarket filly Ribbons. But a fortnight later, Treve was the story again, and this time it was a reverse for Frankie. Scott Burton was the bringer of bad news.

Frankie Dettori was a 'very disappointed' jockey yesterday after learning he is to be replaced by Thierry Jarnet on Treve for the last two outings of the brilliant Arc winner's career.

The shock news is the result of a direct appeal by trainer Criquette Head-Maarek to owner Sheikh Joaan Al Thani to make the switch in the best interests of the filly.

Dettori will be on duty for the sheikh on the Richard Hannon-trained Osaila in the Group 1 Moyglare Stud Stakes at the Curragh

Champagne moment! – at the Shergar Cup in 2014.

on Sunday, while 47-year-old Jarnet partners Treve in the Prix Vermeille as she prepares to defend her Arc crown in the Qatar-backed Longchamp showpiece on 5 October. Al Shaqab Racing manager Harry Herbert told the Racing Post: 'Criquette came to the sheikh and to me too, and she has spoken to Frankie.

'It's a request that Thierry Jarnet gets back on board Treve for these last two races because he gets on very well with her. Not that Frankie doesn't, but Jarnet's with her all the time. It's just Criquette's gut instinct, and she might have only two more bullets to fire with the filly.

'She just feels that, when you're trying to add a percentage here and there, she knows the filly best and would rather Jarnet took the ride.'

Dettori said: 'I have nothing to say on the matter but I am very disappointed and that's it.'

Head-Maarek has been careful to offer no public criticism of Dettori after the previously perfect Treve was beaten at Longchamp and again at Royal Ascot this year, after which the four-year-old was diagnosed with a lumbar injury.

Treve, who was bred and owned by the Head family's Haras du Quesnay before being sold to Sheikh Joaan's Al Shaqab Racing empire last summer, had gone unbeaten on her run to a five-length demolition of what looked a tip-top Arc field last October.

Dettori's sole win on her came in the Vermeille twelve months ago – a considerate ride for which he was praised – before suffering the agony of missing the Arc after breaking a bone in his foot in a fall at Nottingham a few days before Europe's richest race.

Herbert was keen to stress the move does nothing to weaken Al Shaqab's alliance with Dettori, and underlined it was the trainer's direct intervention which led to it.

'Nobody has fallen out, there is no drama, no sackings,' said Herbert. 'It's purely a professional decision taken from within the management and Sheikh Joaan himself, but it's Criquette's decision. This is Criquette saying, "In an ideal world I think it will give the filly that little bit of edge," because he knows her so well and gets on with her brilliantly.'

Following his separation from Godolphin in 2012 and subsequent six-month ban due to a positive test for cocaine, Dettori's career was resurrected by Sheikh Joaan. As recently as last month he was able to celebrate Group 1 success, with his boss in attendance, when scoring on The Wow Signal in the Prix Morny at Deauville.

Indeed, the only blip during Dettori's time as retained rider to Al Shaqab has been Treve's inability to perform at her best when he has been on board this year, although the Prince of Wales's run came with that valid injury excuse.

Herbert added: 'The sheikh has made it quite clear he will do whatever Criquette thinks is best for Treve. It's obviously tough for Frankie, but he is so brilliant, he has taken it in his stride and he understands what is best for the filly and for the organisation.

'While he's immensely disappointed, it is a decision that has been taken – primarily by Criquette – with Treve's best interests at heart. This is not a Frankie and Al Shaqab issue, it's a one-horse scenario, a request from a trainer with a very, very important animal.

'The Arc is absolutely massive for Al Shaqab, for Qatar and for the sheikh. Criquette has been bold enough to step up and ask, knowing there will be PR consequences from these decisions.

'We are lucky to have a great guy in Frankie, who is a team player through and through, and he has been brilliant with what has been tough news for him.'

Submitting to 'The Ice Bucket Challenge' with Clare Balding at York in 2014.

Treve regained her position at the head of the market for the Arc on Sunday following the defeat of Sea The Moon at Baden-Baden, and is a best-priced 9-2 to become the first back-to-back winner of the race since Alleged in 1978.

When Treve and Thierry Jarnet then finished a worrying fourth in the Prix Vermeille, Frankie could content himself that he was not the only jockey to find the great mare disappointing. And even when she came good so gloriously to sprint clear for her second Arc, within the hour Frankie was a winner too, as Bill Barber described.

Olympic Glory put the icing on the cake for Treve's connections and provided a Group 1 success for Frankie Dettori with an extraordinary display.

Slowly away and detached in last early, the Richard Hannon-trained colt weaved his way through the whole field to win going away by two lengths from Gordon Lord Byron.

It was the son of Choisir's fourth success at the highest level.

Hannon said: 'When he missed it five lengths I thought, 'Here we go, what a nightmare'. It was looking shocking and I was a bit worried. I was about to go and get my bag and go home.

'It was one of the strangest races I can remember seeing. It's a most awesome performance and I am very pleased. I must admit I thought the writing was on the wall a long way out.'

Olympic Glory carried the same Al Shaqab colours as Treve, and Sheikh Joaan Al Thani clearly enjoyed the success.

Hannon added: 'I'm absolutely delighted for the sheikh on a day like today. It means a lot to us as an outfit as well. He's unbeaten over seven furlongs, he beat the track record there and he's won a Group 1 for us at two, three and four. He's been a pleasure to be involved with – Dad trained him and now I've trained him. He's been a star.'

Asked about the future for Olympic Glory, Hannon replied: 'Is it his last race? I don't know. He's got a big career at stud ahead of him. Whatever the sheikh decides is what will happen.'

Olympic Glory powers home at Longchamp.

Dettori, who treated the crowd to one of his flying big-race dismounts, admitted he had shared Hannon's concerns in the early part of the race.

'I knew from the form they would go very fast, and the horse likes a fast pace, but I was quite worried because I couldn't keep up and we were a bit detached,' he said. 'After that I felt him go underneath me and the next question was, "How am I going to get through here?"'

There were other reasons for Frankie being in such a sunny mood at Longchamp. He might be turning 44 before Christmas, but he would be doing it with a contract to die for in his pocket, Lee Mottershead wrote.

Frankie Dettori yesterday revealed he had signed a new deal that confirms his position as retained rider to Al Shaqab Racing after a triumphant weekend for the operation highlighted by Treve's magnificent second successive Prix de l'Arc de Triomphe victory.

Dettori lost the mount on Treve at the request of trainer Criquette Head-Maarek, but he secured his boss Sheikh Joaan Al Thani a Group 1 winner at Longchamp on Sunday when steering Olympic Glory to what had, at one point, seemed an unlikely success in the Prix de la Foret.

That performance, combined with the possibility of soft ground on QIPCO British Champions Day, could lead to Olympic Glory, not Toronado, representing Al Shaqab in the Queen Elizabeth II Stakes next weekend, while in the longer term Dettori is looking forward to maintaining an association with an owner for whom he has enjoyed further big-race wins this year on The Wow Signal, Ruler Of The World, Baitha Alga and Osaila.

'Frankie is continuing as Al Shaqab's man and he'll be riding for the sheikh next year,' said racing manager Harry Herbert. 'The deal has been renewed. Sometimes when you buy a fifty per cent stake in a horse the existing owners want to keep the regular jockey on board, but if we buy a horse wholly ourselves Frankie will be riding.

'With Treve, Criquette wanted to use Thierry Jarnet and it was because she was so adamant that we agreed Frankie would not ride. That, however, will not be the norm.'

Dettori, whose commitment to Al Shaqab takes him to Brighton for a single ride this afternoon, said: 'The boss is happy and we've had a great year. It's brilliant for me. I've had four Group 1s and a couple of Royal Ascot wins. That's fantastic. I'm also enjoying riding a lot in France, which some people might not have noticed.

'We are now beginning to develop as a proper superpower. This is a relatively young stable, so it might take us a couple of years yet, but we're getting there. We have mares, we're beginning to have stallions and we've got some nice two-year-olds coming through.

'I'm sure we're going to expand and buy some more nice horses at the sales as well. The boss is a lovely guy to work with, and everyone is very positive.'

Reflecting on missing out on a Treve Arc triumph for the second year running – he was injured last year – Dettori said: 'The way she travelled throughout on Sunday was the Treve of old. When I rode her at Ascot she couldn't lay up – even in the Vermeille she couldn't lay up. Horses aren't machines, but what a great training performance to get her back.'

Frankie could afford the generous words. For he now had a lot more than even the Al Shaqab contract behind him. In November American trainer Wesley Ward booked him to ride and win the Breeders' Cup Juvenile Turf, but it was a phone call a month earlier that had been all-important.

It was from John Gosden. It was made on the day it was announced that John's stable jockey William Buick had been signed up by Godolphin. Back in 1994 it had been John Gosden who launched Frankie on his first great championship season. Now he wanted to work together again. It would herald the greatest year yet.

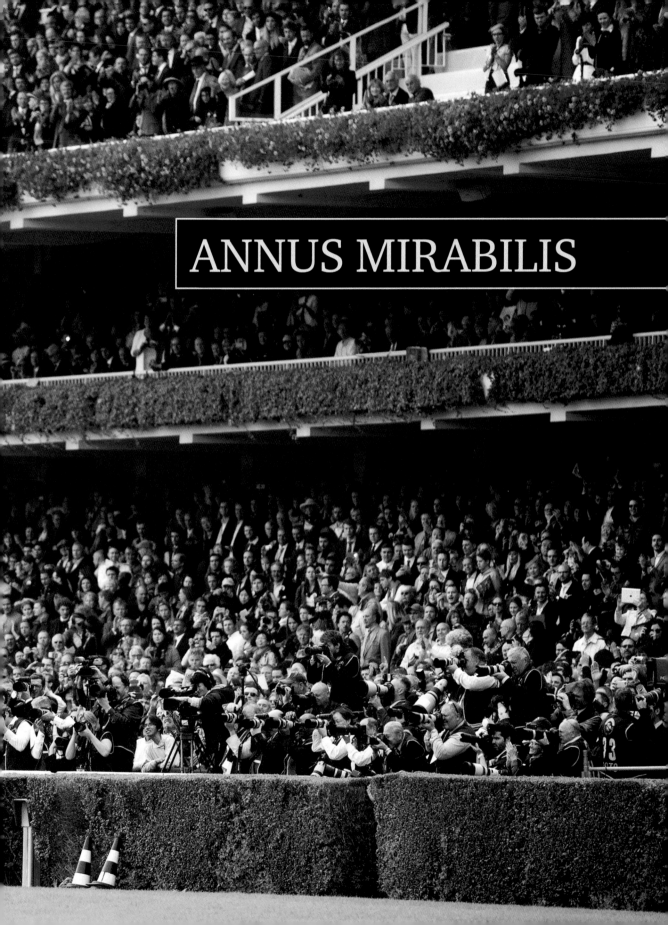

ANNUS MIRABILIS

L ingfield Park on the first Monday in February is not a place normally associated with global megastars. But Frankie was there. So were the first signs that ahead of him was Annus Mirabilis – and Graham Dench picked up the hint.

Frankie Dettori gave a strong indication of how well prepared he is for 2015 when getting down to a weight he managed only twice in domestic competition last year for a maiden win on Wajeeh, who was just his second ride of the year, at Lingfield.

Dettori, who today begins a hectic travel schedule that is likely to keep him out of Britain until next month, put up 1lb overweight at 8st 9lb but said he could have done the 8st 8lb that the Al Shaqab-owned Wajeeh was allotted but for the bitter cold necessitating an extra layer of thermals.

Cold is not going to be an issue where Dettori is going next. He said: 'I'm riding in Qatar on Wednesday and Thursday, Bahrain on Friday, Dubai next week, then Saudi, and probably back to Qatar. I'll see you in March.'

He added: 'I've been working very hard on my fitness and could have done 8st 8lb, but it's so cold today.

Breeder Frankie congratulates jockey Sam Twiston-Davies after Dodging Bullets' victory in the Queen Mother Champion Chase, Cheltenham, March 2015.

'I was due to go to the States to ride Sloane Avenue for Jeremy [Noseda], but it's a handicap and they've given him 8st 2lb. I'm fit, but not that fit!'

Although the record books suggest Dettori has done 8st 8lb and even less a handful of times abroad, including on Treve in the 2013 Prix Vermeille, weighing-out procedures vary in other jurisdictions and he has not done 8st 8lb at home since York in August 2013.

He was lean, fit, hungry and back in demand, on the horse and off it. At the end of February he won the Emir's Trophy on Sheikh Joaan's Dubday, then flew back overnight to ride out and record a pre-Cheltenham piece for Channel 4 Racing at Paul Nicholls' stable in Somerset. Frankie was the breeder of the Nicholls star Dodging Bullets, who duly won at Cheltenham with Frankie trying to look like a jumping man in a brown trilby hat. Back with Flat racing, he was booked as 'ambassador' for the Investec Derby, and closer to home at Newmarket.

The seeds of what was to follow were there on that very first day of the Newmarket season.

Winning the Emir's Trophy in Doha on Dubday, February 2015.

A day after being unveiled as the first official ambassador for Newmarket Racecourses, Frankie Dettori read his own publicity with a double, kicking off with Osaila in the feature Group 3 Lanwades Stud Nell Gwyn Stakes.

Carrying the colours of his backers Al Shaqab, the rider overcame a wide draw on Richard Hannon's filly who was bringing Group 1 form to the table having finished third when last seen at the Breeders' Cup.

The combination stayed on stoutly out of the Dip to beat New Providence by a short head and deny Hugo Palmer a memorable treble after the earlier wins of Gifted Master and Home Of The Brave.

The winner was cut to 16-1 (from 33) for the One Thousand Guineas by most bookmakers after the win and Hannon said: 'I don't know why she was such a big price as she had Group 1 form. Hopefully she can come back here for the Guineas as she'll be better over a mile.'

Dettori then went on to seal his renewed acquaintance with John Gosden when Golden Horn booked a place in next month's Group 2 Dante Stakes at York when accounting for Peacock in the Listed Feilden Stakes.

The son of Cape Cross was cut by Paddy Power to 16-1 (from 25) for the Investec Derby, but winning owner Anthony Oppenheimer said: 'He's not in the Derby and he's not bred to get the trip. He's in the Dante and after that we could look at the French Derby in which he is entered.'

A day later it was announced that Sheikh Joaan's Al Shaqab operation had hired local jockey Gregory Benoist to ride the eighty horses they had in France. It was not a snub but an incentive, as Frankie had a hundred Al Shaqab horses in England to link with the might of John Gosden. In the next ten days he logged a treble at Newbury, beginning with future sprint star Muhaarar in the Greenham, won the Derby trial at Epsom and then rode a four-timer at Sandown, ending with such an impressive win on Jack Hobbs for John Gosden that the three-year-old became Derby favourite.

It was Jack Hobbs that Frankie preferred when stable companion
Golden Horn trounced him in the Dante at York, but by Derby Day all
the stars were again in the rider's favour.
Jon Lees described a famous victory.

Frankie Dettori has been his sport's most recognised face for twenty
years. But in terms of the Investec Derby he was at risk of becoming
just another jockey – until a reunion with mentor John Gosden and
a champion colt in Golden Horn thrust him back into the nation's
hearts yesterday.

He had observed the last three Derbys not from the back of a
horse, but on the television. He had not won a signature European
Group 1 since the 2012 Irish Champion Stakes, and had lost his job
with superpower Godolphin.

Yes! Golden Horn brings Frankie his
second Derby, June 2015.

Yet back on the biggest stage of all the 44-year-old proved he was still box office when he delivered a barnstorming performance, during and after the race, that ensured owner-breeder Anthony Oppenheimer's £75,000 gamble to supplement Golden Horn paid off with the £1.4 million prize.

The responsibility of riding the 13-8 favourite had begun to show in Dettori, whose only previous Derby victory had been eight years ago on Authorized, in the build-up to the race.

But he was coolness personified once it started, settling an initially keen partner towards the back of the field and well adrift of a scorching early pace set by Elm Park and Hans Holbein.

Golden Horn had three behind him exiting Tattenham Corner, but when sent after the leaders two furlongs out he poured on the power, overhauling stablemate Jack Hobbs with a furlong to go and stretching to a three-and-a-half-length win.

Gosden became the third trainer since World War II to claim a Derby 1-2, with Storm The Stars third and Giovanni Canaletto fourth.

An ecstatic Dettori was thankful to an Epsom master for the reassurance he was on the right horse, and a trainer who put him on the first of his twenty Derby mounts.

'I knew this was a good horse. It was up to me to mess it up and everything went right,' he said. 'The reassurance I got just before the race was from Lester [Piggott], who said, "I wish I was on your horse."

'I've had a colourful life and I'm not finished yet. Me and John go back twenty years. I was meant to ride Benny The Dip, he won it, I didn't. Then I won it with Authorized and now finally we've done it together. He's been very constructive in my career, also a friend and father figure, but now I think we're good mates and I'm really enjoying my work this year.'

He added: 'The crowd got Golden Horn a bit excited but the horse wanted to run for me. The first two or three furlongs we slightly had a bit of an argument – that's why I was happy to take him back because he wanted to race too much.

'I was convinced he'd stay but everyone else started to play with my mind a bit. Then I had Giovanni Canaletto in front of me and Jack Hobbs was in front of him, and in my thoughts they were the two to beat. I knew I could beat the others and from there everything went to plan.

'John's last words were, "Be cool, take your time," but at one stage I thought I'd overdone it a bit. He did hit a flat spot but when I gave him a crack he took off, and when I got upsides Jack Hobbs I knew I'd won it. It was shock and relief I'd won the Derby.'

Gosden said: 'Golden Horn was keen out of the gate. I maybe had him a touch fresh but you hate to overdo a horse going into a big race. But Frankie got him covered up and did a lovely job. He put him to sleep and, being an old head, as the others made it a test he didn't panic when they had such a lead on him.

'I said, "Don't press the button till inside the two", and he remembered. It could have been a complete mess if he'd gone too soon or let him roll up with the pace. He did it all right.'

First and second are set to go their separate ways next. The Coral-Eclipse, for which Golden Horn was cut to 6-4 favourite (from 4) by the sponsor, is on his agenda, while Jack Hobbs will head for the Dubai Duty Free Irish Derby.

'If he's in good form and comes out of the race okay, the Eclipse could be a target for Golden Horn,' said Gosden. 'He's not in the Irish Derby.

'Jack Hobbs has done nothing but improve. He's a great big strapping son of Halling. We added him to the Irish Derby and if he's in good form and all right out of this race we'd like to go to the Curragh with him.'

Oppenheimer had not wanted Golden Horn entered in the Derby, believing initially he would not stay, but took little persuading to supplement him after his Dante victory.

Oppenheimer said: 'Once he won at York I didn't take a lot of convincing. At the end of the race he was still going away. He won over nearly a mile and three so it was a no-brainer to go for the best race in the world.

'I've won a Guineas with On The House and one or two other big races, but this is the biggest race in the world. It really is something I've been aspiring to, and my father was aspiring to. It's not easy, it's very difficult. Anything can go wrong and often does, so I'm immensely happy.'

There was so much happiness awash in that winner's enclosure that you wanted to bottle it up for a grumpy day. Alastair Down bottles better than anyone.

This was a fabulous Derby result with everything we needed from this much loved old tart of a Classic, with the two best colts first home on the defining day of John Gosden's career and spiced up by the effervescent resurgence of the world's most loved sardine Frankie Dettori.

Derbys are usually won in the dying stages, but Frankie put this to bed in the first furlong and a half. At 44 he should know a thing or two but all his canniness and experience came into play after Golden Horn came steaming out of the stalls taking a proper hold and plenty keen to have his own way.

In Gosden's words: 'Golden Horn took Frankie on for just over the first furlong but he just said, "No! Come here, go to sleep and do as I tell you."'

If Frankie had not won the argument there and then it could all have got blown to blazes. But hands, brains, strength and sympathy switched Golden Horn's engine telegraph from 'all ahead full' to 'cruise', and within 25 seconds of the start Anthony Oppenheimer's allegedly doubtful stayer was on course for victory.

And never underestimate the human subplots to this race. To us it is the greatest race of the year, a showpiece to be cherished and an equine gunfight fought out over a ludicrous and wicked examination of a racecourse.

But it is also the stuff of drama in terms of the combatants. Twenty years ago Gosden was very much the figure who took the young Dettori in hand and taught him the basics of being a grown-up. Gosden was a second father to Frankie and he has that steadying sort of hand that sees people through the complexities of life.

He didn't make Frankie a saint but he saved him from being a pain in the neck. And the man who knows it most is Dettori himself.

Gosden described the result as being 'beyond wonderful' and to saddle the first two home in the Derby with colts both having their fourth run was wonderful testament to his skills in extracting potential without leaving it behind out of some desperation to get it right on the day.

Two furlongs out it looked as if Jack Hobbs would carry his bat but Dettori, stealthy as a twitcher and only ninth turning for home, had the battle plan for the straight laid out with all the accuracy of an architect's design.

He pulled Golden Horn to the outside with three to run and made his move two out. Leading at the one-pole with both first and second rolling down that punji trap of a camber that has impaled so many final-furlong Epsom hopes, Dettori had the winner rattling and he won by an utterly convincing three and a half lengths.

Needless to say, victory for Dettori brought Epsom to happy boiling point. In my racing lifetime there has never been a man with such a bolted-on connection with the crowd as Frankie. There are dairymen in their late seventies who know less about milking.

And as the only household Flat name since Lester Piggott, Dettori means something to even the most ingenue racegoer. And whereas Lester gave nothing to the public without the exchange of coin of the realm, the sheer joy of triumph on great stages erupts out of Frankie like some force of natural joy.

Most important of all, his enthusiasm is utterly infectious and you would have to be a block of stone not to smile with him. If you didn't enjoy his return to Derby triumph for only the second time and on his first ride for four years, then perhaps you should be following some lesser pursuit.

Everybody from Epsom to Edinburgh got a kiss from Frankie. He knelt on the turf in the winner's enclosure hammering the ground with excitement and screaming 'I can't believe it! Go and find John Gosden as he may have passed out!'

John had done nothing of the sort, of course. Our sport's finest communicator – and he does it for us, not himself – the Big Man, surrounded by family, was just taking it all steadily in.

He is not the high-five sort but he does profound satisfaction very well. At the press conference he wandered in and started talking without a question being asked.

He said he had nearly spoilt both colts when overdoing them on the Limekilns last August and having to leave them alone for a fair bit knowing he had made a hash of it and, possibly, them.

He said he didn't know Jack Hobbs was still okay until the result of him winning his maiden came through from Wolverhampton – of all places – on 27 December.

Gosden said: 'We got the result just as we were finishing our Christmas pudding.'

So one thing learned from Derby Day is that Christmas lunch at the Gosdens is a must as it lasts at least three days!

The other lesson was that, after a run-up when some of us worried this might not be the greatest race, the first two home are very decent at the least.

Presumably Golden Horn will be carded for the likes of the Eclipse and Juddmonte International but there is now no reason to eschew the mile and a half, and full credit to Oppenheimer for having the gumption to go for it.

Today there is every chance we will, as a sport, make some Sunday front pages. So we should, and Golden Horn is something of a gift to headline writers.

Our most famous jockey and a top-class horse have won a sunlit Derby. It was really Gosden who was the founder of the feast and those who occasionally suggest he is fond of the sound of his own voice should reflect that he now has even more to say.

A great day. Classic in every way, shape and, indeed, form.

When Frankie confidence is on the surge he rides the wave with a flair that makes anything seem possible. Within a week of Epsom he and Gosden were at Chantilly to win the French Oaks with Star Of Seville. Within a couple of days he was back in the limelight to ride his fiftieth Royal Ascot winner on Osaila, and follow that with the Tercentenary Stakes on Time Test and the Diamond Jubilee on the American horse Undrafted.

The wave surged on with a great front-running ride on Golden Horn to win the Eclipse at Sandown, a bagpipe procession into the July Course paddock to celebrate his thirty years at Newmarket, and six winners including his sixtieth at the meeting, to clinch the riding title at Glorious Goodwood and lay a long-standing jinx by taking the Stewards' Cup after twenty years of trying.

Fallibility at last got its man at York, when Frankie and Golden Horn allowed the 50-1 shot Arabian Queen too much rope in the Juddmonte International, but a month later they were back in Group 1 action in the Irish Champion Stakes at Leopardstown. Dual Guineas winner

Gleneagles didn't show up, but other pressures certainly did. Jonathan Mullin witnessed an eventful race.

If you thought the Irish Champion Stakes without Gleneagles would be Hamlet without the Prince, you didn't reckon on the race's storied ability to provide drama and intrigue.

Because when the calligrapher sits down to etch Golden Horn's name onto one of European racing's most prized nameplates, the winner's stamp will not expose much of the tale.

But the highlights reel will show the brilliant Derby and Eclipse winner affirming his guts and greatness under Frankie Dettori, being challenged by Free Eagle at the furlong pole, jinking badly right at just the wrong time for his smacked challenger, and going on to beat the running-on Found by a length.

A shadow cast by the grandstand, in a race run an hour and five minutes earlier than stated to enable it to take place on fresh ground, was the most popular 'grassy knoll' put forward by connections for the sudden dive to his right.

'I think it was the shadow of the grandstand and just as the ground gets dark he seems to have run across that line,' said trainer John Gosden. 'He goes very quickly right, Frankie's aware straight away and gives him a slap down the shoulder. I don't know what he saw, he was doing quite nicely up to then.'

As was Free Eagle's trainer Dermot Weld, already on an Irish Champions Weekend double, and who was left ruing what might have been.

'Pat [Smullen] said the interference completely knocked the wind out of Free Eagle and cost him the race,' was Weld's frank assessment. 'But I'm very proud of the horse. I'll speak to Pat, but the Arc has to be under consideration.'

Sitting alongside the drama at Doncaster, it was a big day for stewards, but Found running on well into second and charging past a flailing Free Eagle removed almost all likelihood of Golden Horn being thrown out. And ultimately the stewards took little time before announcing no alteration to the result would be made.

OPPOSITE: Summer highlights in 2015: top, a flying dismount from Osaila at Royal Ascot; and bottom, driving Golden Horn clear of The Grey Gatsby in the Eclipse Stakes.

255

A barging match in the Irish Champion Stakes, but Golden Horn (centre) prevails.

Dettori, for whom the time change had precluded partnering Bondi Beach in the St Leger at Doncaster – who, of course, was the promoted winner in the stewards' room [and subsequently returned to second place] – could be forgiven for adopting a mood devoid of nonsense.

Unlike in the Juddmonte International at York, where Golden Horn had lost his unbeaten record, there was no tactical ambivalence here and Golden Horn kept answering up Leopardstown's deceptively testing straight, his bravery matched only by his class.

'He showed the courage that makes him a real champion,' said Dettori. 'We probably messed up at York but he has a good engine and can do what he wants, so we decided to be positive.'

Gosden said: 'I think he had to do it the hard way, there was no obvious pace in the race and, with a Derby winner, what you didn't want was being boxed in and someone playing with the pace. It was a really good Group 1 run at a proper gallop. He hardly got a breather but he still seemed to be going away at the end.

'He's handled slow ground today but he wouldn't want to see Paris go really soft. He wouldn't run if it did.'

It didn't go soft at Longchamp, and neither did horse or jockey. As Golden Horn completed his preparation, Dettori and Gosden set out their stall for 2016 by winning the Royal Lodge Stakes at Newmarket so impressively with Foundation that he was made Derby favourite, and the Middle Park with Shalaa who looked all over a future champion sprinter and was declared by Frankie as 'the fastest two-year-old I have ever ridden.'

But at Longchamp Golden Horn was seen by locals as only a supporting act to Treve's starring role. After all, she had dazzled in the last two Arcs. The impossible dream was that she should win three.

Lee Mottershead describes a memorable race.

Foundation wins the Royal Lodge Stakes at Newmarket.

They came wanting one result, to see Treve create an extraordinary slice of turf history, but from vast grandstands that will now be bulldozed they instead saw their darling dethroned and glory go to the one man who could prevent this astonishing Arc ending in anti-climax.

Twenty years after his first success in the Prix de l'Arc de Triomphe, Frankie Dettori, still by far the world's most famous jockey, completed his incredible year of renaissance by executing a riding masterclass to notch a decisive victory on Britain's outstanding Derby hero Golden Horn.

Throughout the build-up to this 94th Arc almost all the attention had been on Treve, the seventh dual winner of the €5 million Qatar-backed showpiece but the first to attempt a hat-trick of triumphs. She did so only after connections brought her out of a brief retirement, but the goodbye they had craved did not come, with the red-hot favourite managing only fourth in a contest whose result overflowed with irony.

Two years ago Dettori missed out on capturing a fourth Arc having suffered an injury just days before the race. Last year his opportunity to supplement wins on Lammtarra, Sakhee and Marienbard was scotched when Criquette Head-Maarek persuaded Dettori's employer Sheikh Joaan Al Thani that his highest-profile employee should be removed from Treve's back in favour of Thierry Jarnet.

It was surely therefore with all that in mind that Dettori said: 'It was fate. I could feel it. That's my fourth Arc and it should have been five, maybe six.'

But this was not an occasion when dirty linen was laundered in public, rather an opportunity to celebrate a vanquished but magnificent mare, a superstar colt trained exquisitely by John Gosden, and a mercurial, evergreen jockey whose ride was lauded by Head-Maarek.

'There is no revenge,' said Dettori. 'Treve has been a great mare. I was concentrating only on Golden Horn today and my boss was waiting in the winner's enclosure to give me a high five. Treve has been a revelation these last three years, but I'm thinking of Golden Horn right now.'

For much of this year Dettori has been thinking of an athlete whose owner-breeder Anthony Oppenheimer had two years ago been unable to sell at a price he deemed fair. The son of Cape Cross was unsold at 190,000gns, but yesterday alone he won a first prize of £2.2m to add to the £1.8m he had amassed through victories in the Dante, Derby, Coral-Eclipse and Irish Champion Stakes. There is now just one more chance for him to swell that enormous sum, with

Another whoop and a wave as Golden Horn takes the Prix de l'Arc de Triomphe.

the Breeders' Cup Turf to be considered prior to retirement at Sheikh Mohammed's Dalham Hall Stud.

'I'm thrilled,' said diamond magnate Oppenheimer. 'This transcends money. I have a small stud and he has done it proud.'

To do that he was helped by a masterful ride from Dettori, who initially kept Golden Horn wide from his unfavourable stall 14 draw before slotting in his hard-pulling mount in the slipstream of Treve's pacemaker Shahah.

Treve herself moved into a challenging position, travelling ominously well early in the straight, but at precisely the same time Golden Horn grabbed the lead and surged forward. He passed the post two lengths clear of Flintshire, whose Andre Fabre-trained stablemate New Bay and the now-retired Treve were fractionally further back in third and fourth.

Dettori said: 'I told John this morning, "Listen, I'm not going to spend all the race trying to get in and have him pulling. Leave it to me, I know what I'm doing." He was a bit keen but I've got strong arms and really the race worked out exactly as I thought it would.

'My tactics were good but his performance was unbelievable. Today you saw the real Golden Horn. He put to bed a great Arc field like a real champion. Over the last furlong and a half it would have been impossible for any horse to get near me. I pressed the button and he flew.

'Think of the horses he has beaten, and beaten well. I spent the last furlong enjoying myself. He has given me some tremendous pleasure and is probably the best I've ridden.'

For his part, Gosden, who moved quickly to sign old ally Dettori last autumn after William Buick was hired by Godolphin, described Golden Horn as the best middle-distance Thoroughbred he has trained.

'He is an exceptional athlete, but it is extraordinary both he and Treve went to the sales and nobody wanted them,' said Gosden.

'For all of us this is beyond a dream. To come to the old Longchamp for the last time having witnessed so many wonderful, marvellous Arcs here and to win one ourselves is a dream come true.'

In truth, the dream of most people here failed to be realised. On turf that will remain but in front of grandstands that will not, the Golden Horn team listened with emotion as God Save The Queen played out around l'hippodrome de Longchamp.

We now bid au revoir to the soon-to-be redeveloped racecourse, having said a fond farewell to a queen and saluted some conquering kings.

It was a day for the ages – and for Alastair Down to dip the pen in purple.

An epic of an Arc emphatically skewered by a brilliant colt under a charismatic and brass-bold ride from the legend that is Lanfranco 'Lazarus' Dettori.

Make no mistake, Golden Horn is cut from cloth of gold. If you excise his Juddmonte International defeat from the book – and it was humans who made a hash of the Knavesmire, not him – the Derby winner would be unbeaten.

York looked and felt like a freak result on the day and it should never lessen the esteem in which this colt should be held.

Not only is Golden Horn pure class, he is magnificently hardy, with a herculean work ethic. He has been in serious training since February and for the sort of races he has taken in there is no such thing as a soft preparation.

Those there to be shot at have to have guns put to their heads.

John Gosden's brilliance with Golden Horn has lain in eking out his resources over a long and testing campaign – being tough on him but always leaving another bucket to be hauled up brimful from the well.

Since 1970 the five Derby heroes to come on and win here had no more than five runs, and a couple of them just two and three.

Yesterday was Golden Horn's seventh gig of the season but he looked terrific beforehand, and there isn't a scintilla of doubt he benefited from a tactical masterpiece of a steer.

Drawn wide, Frankie stayed wide early and then, like a precision engineer, floated him across and slotted Golden Horn in seamlessly behind the pacemaker smack in the cat-bird seat.

From that moment on they were free from all the customary Arc scrimmaging and poised like the executioner's axe to deliver the fatal blow.

Gosden described it as a 'gem of a ride', and said: 'Frankie put it in a nutshell to me before the race when he said, "The trouble with the Arc is that they come at you late with arrows." But from the moment he was tracking the pacemaker I was happy with everything.

'Golden Horn is a fabulous horse with a great constitution and a really good mind on him.'

Frankie, elated as only he can be in what must rank as his finest and most vindicating hour, said: 'Drawn wide, I wasn't going to spend all the race trying to get in. Nothing was going to come and get us late.'

Dettori is one of those magicians who could transform the Gobi Desert into the Garden of Eden and in a sense that is what he has done with his career. There have been a few nights of doubt and sorrow but he has weathered the dire days and frankly it is a pleasure to have him restored in every way to his rampant best.

And somewhere along the line the superficiality and silliness has found its level. He still milks a win and entertains everyone hugely, but you sense his satisfaction runs deeper and is more profound.

Maybe it is the sobering prospect of five sets of school fees – or perhaps he has achieved a sense of balance within himself. It is good to see because he remains the public's favourite jockey of the last 25 years and to have him back in the ascendant is a boon for us all.

At 44, he is proof that most jockeys get better as they get older because all that experience and accumulated wisdom can be brought to bear instantly and at will.

And if you want a testament to his ability it came from racing's favourite grandmother, Criquette Head-Maarek, who could be forgiven for having more pressing concerns than paying tribute to Frankie after Treve's honourable eclipse in a fine fourth place.

She said: 'Frankie rode a remarkable race and it was no disgrace to be beaten and there are no excuses. Watching the replay it struck me what a fantastically intelligent ride Frankie produced today.'

Today they start mothballing Longchamp ahead of the wrecking ball's trundle in to knock down the old and usher in the new.

Many would have liked this day to have produced the first triple winner of the Arc, but it may be just and right that the seven dual winners remain equal.

And in Golden Horn we have an utterly deserving and genuinely great winner of what was a fabulous finale for the old course as we have known and loved it.

Two weeks after the Arc, the UK season held its final gala with QIPCO Champions Day at Ascot and in perfect reflection of their season together he and John Gosden teamed up on a horse called Flying Officer to win the opening race of the meeting, the QIPCO British Champions Long Distance Cup. What's more, it was won by a piece of inspired opportunistic riding up the inside rail more than half a mile from home which would never have come from the fading embers of talent that was Frankie Dettori a few

Flying Officer draws first blood on British Champions' Day at Ascot.

years ago. It was his 72nd winner and took his UK prize money past £4.8 million, higher than in any of his former glory years.

If there was a sense of satisfaction in the portrait Lee Mottershead penned in the Racing Post that Sunday, it was a deserved one.

Across a wall in the kitchen of Frankie Dettori's home near Newmarket is a long line of colourful rosettes. Every one of them has been won this year by his children. From left to right are prizes given for victories in show jumping, polo and other horsey endeavours, while on a table a few feet away are two rather impressive prizes given this year to the head of the household. The kids have done well these last few months but so, too, has their old man.

When visitors have popped by, Dettori has shown off the trophies with pride, one of them presented after the Investec Derby, the other following the Qatar Prix de l'Arc de Triomphe. Both races were won by the horse he describes as probably the best he has ridden, Golden Horn, the willing and exceptionally able Thoroughbred who has been the equine highlight of his rider's incredible campaign.

We are not emu-sed. Frankie at home with his emu Cheep-Cheep, 2015.

Should Hollywood ever tell the story of Dettori's life they would probably now call filming to a halt. So astonishing has been the year, and so striking the reversal in Dettori's fortunes, this might seem the perfect place to stop. But Dettori is not finished. He almost was finished, less than three years ago when his career and reputation were in tatters. Yet he has returned, louder, bolder, more vibrant, charismatic and brilliant than ever.

He greets us in a grey dressing gown then leaves briefly to change into a crisp shirt and trousers. On his return we enter a room in which the heating has been turned up high to help Colm O'Donoghue sweat off a couple of pounds while walking on a treadmill. On this occasion Dettori has no weight worries, so he leaves his perspiring friend and prepares a late breakfast of yoghurt, nuts and honey. The honey, acquired from the Middle East, costs £150 a tub, while the dish is assembled inside a fancy cocktail glass. Frankie, as ever, has his own somewhat over-the-top way of doing things.

It is a way that has worked wonderfully well. The job Sheikh Joaan Al Thani gave Dettori in the summer of 2013 has served them both nicely, but even more crucial to the Sardinian's extraordinary season has been former boss John Gosden. As a result of William Buick teaming up with Dettori's long-time employer Godolphin (the irony is lost on no one) the 44-year-old has worked this year as first jockey to a trainer who has supplied him not only with Golden Horn but also seven of his eight 2015 Group 1 triumphs. His mounts in Europe have won in the region of £8 million. No wonder, then, words like revival, renaissance and resurgence keep being used.

'Yeah, yeah, all that crap,' says Dettori, but you know he sees it in exactly the same way as everyone else.

'It has possibly been my best ever year, but basically I landed on my feet. Sheikh Joaan gave me a lifeline and then last year I got the call from John, who is brilliant, saying (in a fine impression of Gosden), "Hello, matey. I've got a plan."

'The first year I'm back with John and he's only gone and got Golden Horn! What an amazing year we've had but there have been a few near misses, too. We were beaten a nose in the King George, a neck in the Juddmonte and a head in the Opera, so it could have been even better.

'The whole thing is fate. There is no explanation to it. When I think about the year I've had, even I don't really understand it. It has been mental. I had my fiftieth Royal Ascot winner and who do I beat in a photo? My old boss. You couldn't make it up.'

Given he was competing against his current boss, the Arc was quite unusual. Sheikh Joaan was trying to make history with Treve, but with Dettori last year replaced on the mare, he was aboard Golden Horn, on which a wide draw proved no barrier to glory.

'Believe it or not, I was quite confident,' he says. 'From my draw I had to make up the ground slowly. When I eventually went to come across they all dropped back and let me in. I thought, "Jesus Christ! They're giving this race to me!" Then I was saying to myself, "Wait for the corner, wait for the corner!" I had told John when we got to the top of the straight I would be off because they would be coming at me like arrows. But they didn't come because he was absolutely flying.

'Take out the Treve angle and all the British people there were rooting for me. It's very rare you can hear people screaming while you're riding in a race but I could hear them as we went past the furlong marker. I knew then I was going to win as I knew they were screaming for me.

'After the race I was trying to find my son, Leo. I had special permission to take him out of school at Stowe. We went on the jet together, we had breakfast together and then I had a sweat in the bath while he was messing about with his computer. He is part of my life and he was part of that day.

'I started looking for him in the winner's enclosure. I was shouting his name and I carried on shouting it when I got in the carriage because I wanted him to come out with me for the ceremony. His mates had given him money to put on Golden Horn and it turned out he was collecting all their winnings. He ended up with more money than me!

'To be honest, I'm probably more like a big brother to my kids than a father. They call me Dad but they don't see me as Dad. I'm more silly than they are. A father is usually a serious person with their kids, but I'm not like that. They probably think I'm absolutely nuts.'

Dettori's relationship with his own father was very different. Gianfranco Dettori was a riding legend in Italy but at home he was a strict, demanding disciplinarian who sent his young son to Newmarket and left him there while he cried homesick tears.

Now their relationship is much stronger, although for an all too long period during Dettori's twenties it was non-existent. They came together again as a result of the terrible accident in 2000 that cost pilot Patrick Mackey his life.

'I didn't speak to my father for two years,' says Dettori. 'We had a big argument. All hell broke loose. Everything blew out of proportion and it ended up with him not wanting to speak to me and me not wanting to speak to him. Then there was the plane crash.

'Nobody knows when they're going to die. I was nearly there. When the time did come all I could think was, no, not now. I've just got going, I've just got married. I thought I was going to die, 100 per cent. I wasn't screaming or anything like that. I was just so disappointed I was going to die.

'After it happened Dad came over, we both said sorry and that was that. If it weren't for the plane crash we still wouldn't be speaking to each other. He came to see me and said life was for living, not for arguing about stupid things.'

Dettori senior still comes to visit his son, daughter-in-law Catherine and the couple's five children. In future he will turn up at a different property for the Dettoris are selling their Stetchworth home, in one corner of which is the DJ equipment the three-time

The Diamond Jubilee Stakes

More highlights of 2015: with HM The Queen after winning the Diamond Jubilee Stakes at Royal Ascot on Undrafted; and opposite, celebrating fifty Royal Ascot winners.

champion jockey performs from at his famous parties, the most recent of which came on the night of Golden Horn's Arc. Two years from now the Dettoris will be living in a new home across Newmarket on land close to the family stud. The house has yet to be built, but following a year like this one the finances should not be a problem.

'We've lived here for eighteen years but I have nothing to do with this house,' says Dettori. 'The house is the woman's kingdom. Whatever she wants to do is good enough for me. I love it here but it will be just as nice in the new place.'

In recent years Dettori has become familiar with moving. For much of his career the one-time captain on *A Question of Sport* was first jockey to Godolphin and inextricably linked to the organisation. They parted in October 2012 after an eighteen-year association during which Sheikh Mohammed's stable enjoyed enormous success.

The reasons for the split have been well documented. Dettori was forced to share rides with Mickael Barzalona and Silvestre de Sousa. He found it increasingly humiliating and wanted out. The Arc, a race that treated him so kindly this year, had been similarly helpful in 2012.

'My head was fried,' he says. 'I couldn't see the end of it but then God sent me Camelot. He really was a godsend because taking the ride on a Ballydoyle horse in the Arc gave me an excuse to go. I remember Michael Tabor saying to me: "You know what's going to happen if you ride this horse" I said I knew exactly what was going to happen and that was the reason I wanted to ride him. That horse was my ticket out of Godolphin and I grabbed it with both hands.

'We terminated things quite well. We didn't slag each other off and apart from the last eighteen months it was a great relationship. I still say hello to Sheikh Mohammed but that's about it.'

Hot on the heels of the Godolphin separation was a six-month drugs ban and, not quite as embarrassingly, an appearance on *Celebrity Big Brother*. When he returned nobody seemed to want him. Dettori, the man who in 1996 had made headlines around the world thanks to his Ascot 'Magnificent Seven', floundered. He carried on floundering until Sheikh Joaan decided he did want him. A long and successful union seems likely.

'I was so close to retiring,' he says. 'I didn't want to retire but there was nothing out there for me. Nothing. Then Sheikh Joaan restarted me.

'I'm getting more of a buzz out of this job because it's all new. It was the same when I started with Godolphin in the nineties. It's very fresh. Sheikh Joaan is a young man but he is not stupid. He knows what's going on and he loves it. That's a good combination.

'We only began three years ago but we've already made some stallions and we've got a champion racemare. They are buying yearlings and they've started breeding. It doesn't happen overnight. Sheikh Mohammed has been doing it for forty years. We've been doing it for three years but already in that short time so much has been achieved. I can see this becoming a proper outfit like all the other superpowers.

'I'm also looking at the bigger picture. I feel great right now. My belief is the mind carries the body. If your mind is in a good place your body follows it. I'll get to fifty as a jockey, no problem. After that, I don't know. After fifty, every year is borrowed. I can't ride for ever and hopefully when I finish I'll have a managerial and advisory role with Al Shaqab. Even if it's not in the saddle I'll have a lot to offer.'

Right now he is satisfying *Racing Post* photographer Edward Whitaker by moving around the house for different pictures, including one close to the indoor cage in which Huffy the hedgehog lives. 'You know what to do,' says Whitaker. 'Pose, hands, hands. Now engage.' Putting on a soft, arty accent, Dettori repeats: 'Engage.' Whitaker clicks away before imploring of his subject: 'Don't smile. No, not sullen, either.' Dettori swears at Whitaker.

Indeed, this Italian import has within his repertoire a fine range of English expletives, which he uses liberally but with good effect, as he does phrases like 'hunky-dory' and 'belly-up', which is what he says happened to the restaurants that bore his name. Before the eateries went belly-up, and while they and the range of Frankie's pizzas and ice cream existed, they provided a good representation of his fame and celebrity. Yet Dettori would be the first to admit the effervescent man you see on TV screens is not necessarily an altogether accurate representation of the real him.

'I am what I am and I try not to change,' he says. 'I have never treated myself as famous, although I get recognized a lot. It has been happening all my life. From the age of nineteen I've had this following. There are times when I enjoy it and times when I don't.

'I have highs and lows. My wife and family know when to avoid me. I am definitely an up-and-down person. I know that. I also know I can be moody. Everyone says that about me and they can't all be wrong.'

The highs could be partly influenced by the strong espresso coffee he enjoys drinking. He finishes another cup and starts to lead us out of the kitchen and past walls on which are adorned pictures that tell remarkable stories.

'The big things in my life,' says Dettori, 'the things that changed the course of my life, were the 'Magnificent Seven', the plane crash and leaving Godolphin. They were the huge things.

'When I look back at my life it has been mad. It has been extremely colourful as well. I wouldn't change anything. Even all the bad things that happened have shaped my life and shaped me into what I am now. You need to have your good times but you also have to make mistakes. There are a lot of things I've done wrong but I don't regret having done them.

'I'm not finished yet, either. I have a lot more still to achieve. There are lots of races I've never won like the Melbourne Cup, Champion Stakes and July Cup. I'll try my best to win them. But as a professional jockey winning the Derby on Golden Horn was the biggest thrill I've ever had. Nothing compares to that.'

That was a victory, and this has been a year, that reinforced Frankie Dettori's status as the world's most famous jockey. Before Ryan Moore started dominating the sport, Dettori was also regarded by many to be the world's best jockey. Nearly thirty years into his career, and once again riding on the crest of a wave, does he consider himself to be as good as anyone?

'Oh yeah,' he says with certainty. 'You've got to have self-belief. Never, not once, did I stop believing in myself. Otherwise, why would I have come back? The great thing is I was up there, I lost it and then I came back. This time it's twice as sweet.'

The pint-sized fifteen-year-old who cried himself to sleep in Newmarket thirty years ago is a very different creature now. The aspiring jockey who wrote 'Frankie goes to Hollywood' on tissue paper as he was driven home from that first British winner at Goowood in 1987 has now circled the globe near on a thousand times.

He has been to the highest peaks, has looked death, disgrace and disaster in the face, and has come back to climb even higher yet. On his way he has become the best known jockey in history and has brought a unique Latin zest to an often staid old game.

There are still winters and summers to come, but when it's over he will have left an imprint like none other. He has not just galloped at life, he has added to it.

Frankie: The Riding Record

Compiled by John Randall (to 29 October 2015)

- **Born** 15 December, 1970
- **Apprenticed to** Luca Cumani, Newmarket 1987–9
- **First winner** Rif, Turin, 16 November 1986
- **First winner in Britain** Lizzy Hare, Goodwood, 9 June 1987
- **Lost claim** Versailles Road, Beverley, 18 July 1989
- **First Group winner** Legal Case (1989 Select Stakes)
- **First Group 1 winner** Markofdistinction (1990 Queen Elizabeth II Stakes)
- **Derby winners** Authorized (2007), Golden Horn (2015)
- **Dubai World Cup winners** Dubai Millennium (2000), Moon Ballad (2003), Electrocutionist (2006)
- **Prix de l'Arc de Triomphe winners** Lammtarra (1995), Sakhee (2001), Marienbard (2002), Golden Horn (2015)
- **King George VI and Queen Elizabeth Stakes winners** Lammtarra (1995), Swain (1998), Daylami (1999), Doyen (2004)
- **Japan Cup winners** Singspiel (1996), Falbrav (2002), Alkaased (2005)
- **Breeders' Cup Classic winner** Raven's Pass (2008)
- **Breeders' Cup Turf winners** Daylami (1999), Fantastic Light (2001), Red Rocks (2006), Dangerous Midge (2010)
- **Other Breeders' Cup winners** Barathea (1994 Mile), Wilko (2004 Juvenile), Ouija Board (2006 Filly & Mare Turf), Donativum (2008 Juvenile Turf), Pounced (2009 Juvenile Turf), Hootenanny (2014 Juvenile Turf)
- **Other British Classic winners** Balanchine (1994 Oaks), Moonshell (1995 Oaks), Classic Cliche (1995 St Leger), Mark Of Esteem (1996 2,000 Guineas), Shantou (1996 St Leger), Cape Verdi (1998 1,000 Guineas), Island Sands (1999 2,000 Guineas), Kazzia (2002 1,000 Guineas, Oaks), Scorpion (2005 St Leger), Sixties Icon (2006 St Leger), Conduit (2008 St Leger), Blue Bunting (2011 1,000 Guineas)
- **Queen Elizabeth II Stakes winners** Markofdistinction (1990), Mark Of Esteem (1996), Dubai Millennium (1999), Ramonti (2007), Poet's Voice (2010)
- **7 winners on one card** Ascot, 28 September 1996
- **Champion apprentice** 1989
- **Champion jockey** 1994, 1995, 2004
- **Most wins in a British season** 233 (1994)